BUILD YOURSELF
WITHOUT LIMITS

A Strategy To Win In All Areas Of Your Life!

ANDREW DEUTSCH

Build Yourself Up Without Limits - A Strategy to Win In All Areas of Your Life !

Copyright © 2020 by Andrew Deutsch

All rights reserved. Published in the United States. No part of this book may be used or reproduced in any manner whatsoever without written permission, except in the case of brief quotations em- bodied in critical articles or reviews.

This book is a work of fiction. Names, characters, businesses, organizations, places, events and incidents either are the product of the author's imagination or are used fictitiously. Any resemblance to actual persons, living or dead, events, or locales is entirely coincidental.

For information contact :

Andrewdeutsch9@gmail.com http:/andrewdeutsch.net

Book and Cover design by Designer

ISBN: 9798558993035

First Edition: November 2020

ACKNOWLEDGEMENTS

The first person I want to thank is Phillip Engel, who is an awesome uncle - he always has gone the extra mile and a half for me! I also want to thank his children, Wendy, Terri, Elise and Steven, and of course, his wonderful wife, Margie, who have always been like family to me. I want to thank my father, Eliezer, and my brothers, Alon and Roni Deutsch, in Israel, for their love and support. I want to additionally thank Deb Burns who believed in this book from the start.

TABLE OF CONTENT

Introduction 1

Chapter 1: The Character Actor Voices In Your Head That Will Lie And Beat You Up! 3

    The Common Character Actor Voices In Our Heads 3

    Chapter 1 Summary 8

Chapter 2: You're Shoulding Yourself! 9

    Why Is It That Nobody Ever Says "I Really Built Myself Up Today?" 10

    Tyranny Of Shoulds 10

    Sound Familiar? 11

    Chapter 2 Summary 12

Chapter 3: Your Shame Committee (And How It Began) 14

    We Were Shamed By Our Parents, And Now We Shame Ourselves 14

    Top Ten List Of Bad Childhood Experiences 16

    Chapter 3 Summary 18

Cbhapter 4: I Suck Radio 19

    Examples Of Toxic Voices From The Past 19

    It Starts In The Morning 21

    Why Do We Keep Tuning Into Toxic Radio? 21

    Chapter 4 Summary 22

Chapter 5: A Spiritual Solution – Are You Kidding Me? 23

    Thought-Based Solutions 23

    Event: 24

The Solution Is Spiritual 26

What Is The Spiritual Condition? 26

What Is The Emotional Condition? 27

Chapter 5 Summary 28

Chapter 6: Museum States ™ 30

"Museum States" ™ Are Mind Apps 31

Museum States ™ Exhibit Listing 33

The Crumbaholic ™ 33

Edge-Meister ™ 34

The Control Freak ™ 34

Mr. Or Ms. Guilty 35

The Perfectionist ™ 35

The Snobaholic ™ 36

The Nitpicker 36

Angst-Glutton ™ 37

The Panicker 37

Struggleaholic ™ 38

The Misery-Maven ™ 38

The Crises King Or Queen ™ 38

The Lessthaner ™ 39

The Worrier ™ 39

The Rageaholic ™ 39

The Pleaser ™ 40

The Gloom And Doomer ™ 40

The Superhuman ™ 41

The Eggshell Walker ™ 41

Chapter 6 Summary 46

Chapter 7: The Power Of Spiritual Energy 48

Using Spiritual Energy To Dial-Back Beating Yourself Up 51

God Shots 53

Your God Shot Story: 55

Imagination 56

Persistence 56

The Reliability And Functioning Of Our Bodies 56

Inherited Cultural Instincts And Disciplines 57

Sense Of Humor 57

Intelligence 58

Mindfulness 58

Love 58

Talents 58

What's My Part? 60

Chapter 7 Summary 60

Chapter 8: "Powerfirmations™" **62**

Powerfirmations™ For Acknowledging The Small And Big Things We Do 62

"Good Job!" 63

"I'm Proud Of Me!" 64

"More God's Success Than Mine" 64

The Art Of Powerfirmations™ 64

The Art Of Powerfirmations™ Is A Healthy Discipline 67

Self-Care Is God's Care 69

Chapter 8 Summary 69

Chapter 9: Hey, You Can Leave Your Position As The Curator Of Your Museum States™! **71**

How To "Spot And Catch" A Museum State™ 71

For Being A Lessthaner™ 73

For Being A Struggleaholic™ Or An Angst-Glutton™ 73

For Being A Crumbaholic™ Or A Misery-Maven™ 73

For The Worrier 73

For The Gloom And Doomer™ 73

For The Panicker ™ 74

For The Crises King Or Queen 74

For The Superhuman 74

For The Eggshell Walker ™ 74

For Mr. And Ms. Guilty 74

For The Edge-Meister ™ 74

For The Perfectionist 75

For The Snobaholic ™ 75

For The Control Freak 75

For The Rageaholic 75

For The Pleaser 75

For The Nitpicker™ 76

What Kind Of Story Are You Telling Yourself? 76

Creating A Combination Powerfirmation™ 77

Let Me Eat Crumbs? 78

Mini-Powerfirmations™ 80

Transit Vehicles 82

Beating Yourself Up 82

Sand-Trap Thinking 82

Negative Endowment 83

Compare And Despair 83

Screenwriting 84

The Jack Screenplay 84

The Power Of Objectivity 87

Chapter 9 Summary 88

Chapter 10: A Conversation Without Condemnation! 90

Reactive Response: 92

Relational Response: 92

Conversations With Condemnation And Without Condemnation 93

Components Of The Conversation Without Condemnation 94

Follow-Up Conversation Without Condemnation 98

Chapter 10 Summary 101

Chapter 11: Build A Relationship - Not A Reactiveship™! ... 103

Are You On Thinking Terms With Yourself? 105

Reactive Thoughts 106

Reactiveship Behavior 108

Showing Up Late Story 109

Don't Override Your Gut Reaction! 110

Two Brains? Who Knew! 111

Just God Gps It! 111

How To Find The God Voice Within You 114

Use God Gps For Thinking! 115

Persistence And Love Within A Spiritual Condition 117

Relationship Stories 117

No Socks Story At The Wedding 117

God Gps For Choosing Relationships 118

Chapter 11 Summary 119

Chapter 12: Grow A Lush Spiritual Garden In Your Mind! 121

Going From Weedy Thoughts To Garden Thoughts 121

Weedy Pictures And Garden Pictures 125

Going From Weedy Choices To Garden Choices 128

A Vigilant Gardener 131

Chapter 12 Summary 132

Chapter 13: Your Life With And Without Powerfirmations .. 134

Life Situation 1 135

Without Powerfirmations 135

With Powerfirmations 136

Life Situation 2 137

Without Powerfirmations 137

With Powerfirmations 139

Life Situation 3 140

Without Powerfirmations 140

With Powerfirmations 141

Life Situation 4 142

Without Powerfirmations 142

With Powerfirmations 143

Life Situation 5 144

Without Powerfirmations™ 144

With Powerfirmations 145

Life Situation 6 147

Without Powerfirmations 147

With Powerfirmations 148

Life Situation 7 149

Without Powerfirmations 149

With Powerfirmations 150

Illness Or Injury 152

Powerfirmations For The Judge And Lawyer 153

Chapter 13 Summary 156

Chapter 14: Achieve Your Goals And Aspirations Using Powerfirmations! **157**

Share And Develop Your Talents 157

Talent Inventory 158

Just Change One Thing A Day 161

The Basis Of Positive Change 162

Overcoming Resistance To Change Or Growth 164

How Old Are You? 164

God, I Now Take The Limits Off Of You! 165

The I Should Be Now Report Card 169

Preventive Powerfirmations 171

Fear Of Rejection By A Decision-Maker 173

The Not Too Structured Daily Goals List 173

Chapter 14 Summary 177

In Conclusion (For Now) 179

Will Fade Away, Unless You Give It Away! 181

INTRODUCTION

Why don't you live your life joyfully and energized? Is the problem the government, technology, or society at large? No, the problem is that you spend much more time beating yourself up rather than building yourself up and you've been doing it so long that most of the time you're not even aware that it's happening! Why is that? Well, for one thing, it feels like home.

Think of it this way, you're at home and it's run-down, you get yelled at a lot, and don't feel good most of the time. One day you make new friends, and they encourage you to spend less time at your home and more time with them. Their home is beautiful with well-kept lawns, a swimming pool and tennis courts. You feel out of place, uncomfortable, and your desire to be with these people is strong, but so is the fear that tries to stop you at every turn. That's why it takes courage. You will be leaving something familiar even though it isn't good for you, and replacing it with something unfamiliar that is a million times better!

This book is about helping you to leave your "run-down home" and spend more and more time in a "mansion." You will be given the tools to build yourself up without limits. To change how you relate to yourself is about becoming a new person, a person you've never been. Take this exciting journey with me, and each exercise you do will help you get there.

I did not have a good or happy childhood. I was raised in a home with a mother who had severe mental health problems. My father left our home and lived in a foreign country. After many years of therapy, fifteen years ago I began to work with clients as a life coach and I also spoke to groups. About ten years ago I began leading workshops in the United States and around the world.

I found that one rule never changes: To stop a bad behavior, it has to be replaced with a good behavior that is a high-quality replacement. You can't stop bad behavior and replace it with nothing. One good behavior that will be suggested in this book is "for you to keep the good you've acquired; you have to give it away." Why? It's about the awesome power of helping others.

You are not an island. You need others to get the maximum value from this book. It's really easy: Read the book, do the exercises, integrate this book into your life so that you are actually living it, and share what you have learned with as many trusted friends as you can! When you help others, they become a battery-boost for you to tap the power of unlimited positive spiritual energy!

Many of us at some point in our lives have the belief that our situation is too far gone to be bettered. In this book, you will learn that rarely is this the case if you use the appropriate tools to improve your situation. I have seen many situations that looked hopeless that have positively turned around through the use of the tools in this book. This has been true for my own life, which looked bleak to me until I developed these ideas and created these tools. Today, I live a prosperous and happy life and help people build themselves up without limits!

This is serious stuff, and the way I deal with serious stuff is to not take it too seriously! I hope you enjoy reading this book and becoming the person who builds themselves up without limits to win!

Chapter 1

The Character Actor Voices in Your Head That Will Lie and Beat You Up!

Micro-addictions? I know, you're probably saying "You've got to be kidding! I never heard that!" I know most people never think about micro any-thing with the exception of a microwave oven! Most of the times when we hear our friends talk about any addictions, if they're not referring to major addictions such as to drugs or alcohol, they mean their inability to stop certain less harmful habits such as checking their e-mail 10 times during their family dinner. But beating ourselves up is also a micro-addiction! So, when we are beating ourselves up, down or sideways, we are doing our drug.

There are basic voices that most of us have in our heads which we live with every day which during specific situations will sound very real and try to convince us to believe them. They are the common voices of beating ourselves up.

The Common Character Actor Voices in Our Heads

Whether you want to call it resistance, our disease, our lower self, or the enemy within, it has many ways of showing up in our lives that are very tricky. In fact, it is cunning and baffling. It assumes many internal character actor voices, and its agenda is to always stop us from evolving, risking, loving or simply being visible. In short, these are voices that can undermine us. They lie to us and beat us up! If they win, our consequence will be to feel empty or miserable. These voices are caused by fear that is part of the hard-drive of our minds.

The following are examples of how these voices in you assume different characters. Are they familiar to you? At the end of this section, I suggest you write out any recurring character voices that you've heard in your head for years that I listed and any additional characters that I didn't list.

Here are some of the characters in the "dressing room" of my mind and the minds of my clients, and maybe they are in your own mind too!

The Slacker Voice: "Dude, don't work on the book; you're too tired!"

The Smothering Mother/Father Voice: "Don't go to the networking event - you'll catch a cold! Also, eat, eat, eat - you're so skinny. You're only 280 pounds!!!"

The Critical Father/Mother/Teacher Voice: "You didn't do it right. It's not good enough. You are so lazy! You probably shouldn't try again; you don't have what it takes! Don't forget the classic, "Why can't you do it as well as your sister or brother?

The Lawyer Voice: "What are the odds of you succeeding? I'd say slim to none. Others have tried and failed. Do you really think you're better than they are? I'm just giving you this advice so you don't waste your money and time!"

The Prosecutor Voice: "Remember all the times you failed in trying to reach your goal. The evidence is against you. Don't waste your time trying again, because you failed too many times. It doesn't matter that some people say you have good ability in this area. They're just wrong!"

The Cruel Condemner Voice: "You are a total (fill in with your favorite insult – e.g. loser). You don't deserve any good in your life!"

The Redneck Voice: "Honey, you are so ugly - your face is like eight miles of bad road!"

The Judge Voice: "I sentence you because of what you did or didn't do, or said or didn't say. In short: You're guilty!"

These are archetypes, but they can blend and meld into another.

Here are some examples of hybrid character actor voices.

A Critical Father Judge.

A Smothering Mother Slacker.

A Redneck Cruel Condemner.

Now, please fill in your common beating yourself up character actor voices:

1. _____

2. _____

3. _____

4. _____

5. _____

6. _____

7. _____

8. _____

9. _____

10. _____

11. _____

As always, share these character actor voices with a trusted friend, and ask them to share theirs with you!

Behaviors Caused by These Character Actor Voices

These voices encourage unhealthy behavior which gives us reason to beat ourselves up even more! Here are some examples of the behaviors these character actor voices cause:

We're too tired – time to zone-out!

We tell ourselves we're tired when we're not, and then fall asleep or zone out. This is usually done when we want to avoid a delayed gratification experience such as writing a book or a doctoral thesis, making a business plan or especially working out!

You know that's you, at least when it comes to working out!

We blew the deadline!

We set up deadlines when no deadline is required. This is cunningly done so we can attack ourselves when we don't complete the work by a deadline that didn't need to be there to begin with! What we're really doing is setting ourselves up to relive old angst, "living on the edge" and "feeling less than."

The attack of the too!

We are critical of ourselves, so we avoid intimacy, risk, even fun! This usually creates the "too" structure in you: "You're too old;" "You're too ugly;" "You've been single too long;" "You've been alone too long;" and everybody's favorite lie: "It's too late!"

We just can't find the time!

We don't connect with something we love to do even for five

minutes a day because we tell ourselves "we don't have time" or "other things are more important" like watching the news!

We can't stop ourselves from multi-tasking!

We scroll through our cell phones, keep reading our email or have fixations on social media and internet browsing rather than appreciating the moment, the thought, or nature. This can be detrimental to our emotional and physical health. Triple the danger if we're texting while driving!

Hey, let's pig out, to numb out!

How about binging on cinnamon buns with a strawberries & crème malt or worse! Then, the Condemner comes out of the "dressing room" again and says "Look at you! You're a fat slob!" "You wouldn't want me to repress my feelings, would you?"

Being emotionally reactive!!!! We yell first, and ask questions later.

The Underlying Causes of These Behaviors

What these behaviors have in common is that they all start with fear! Fear of losing what we have and not getting what we want, and then beating ourselves up, acting out, acting in, not acting, or acting and not valuing what we're doing. Besides fear, they also are produced by our being selfish, inconsiderate, and dishonest with ourselves, our family, friends, and community. As I discussed in Chapter 5, these shortcomings operate like boomerangs, we fling them out, and they come back to whack us in the head!

So Now What?

At this point you're probably saying "I sort of knew that, but sort of didn't, but what else is there about this beating ourselves up business that I don't know?" Glad you asked! In working with clients over the years a series of patterns in their life emerged again and again that created and recreated new problems for them. They were always based on how they felt most of the time growing up as children. As my clients talked more about the ways they beat themselves up, it became clear they were unconsciously recreating these states in their lives and were creating unnecessary difficulty in achieving their goals or just living their lives. There are many terms for these recurring behaviors that are all over the internet. However, the problem is that these terms are not "practically transportable" to be used in your daily life.

Let's move ahead into Chapter 7 and look at how these states come alive in you. I call them "Museum States ™."

Chapter 1 Summary

- Beating ourselves up internal voices are micro-addictions.

- There are common actor voices in our heads that lie to us and beat us up.

- These voices are caused by fear that is part of the harddrive of our minds.

- If left unchecked, these voices encourage unhealthy behavior, which gives us reason to beat ourselves up even more!

Chapter 2

You're Shoulding Yourself!

"If we don't build ourselves up without limits, we will beat ourselves up without limits." magine a relationship with a friend, lover, mother, father, sister, brother, or cousin. This person insults you every day, lies to you, says you do not measure up in everything you I do.

These insults create barriers to stop you from taking healthy risks. What's worse is you never think *even once, of ending this relationship*!

This is an example of how you live with you now:

You wake up at three in the morning to get a glass of water. As you're walking to the refrigerator, a voice says to you: "Hey, the loser just got up!" Or perhaps while you're drinking the water, you're thinking about a task for the day. Perhaps, today you're thinking about auditioning for a play. The role could be as small as a spear carrier in a Greek tragedy.

Another voice says "they will never cast you!" It's as if sometimes your mind has nothing better to do then put you down. This is no way for you to live!

Amazingly, this is the one activity everyone has plenty of time for! Did you ever hear someone say, "You know pal, I just don't have enough time to beat myself up anymore!"

Maybe they say that on the planet Saturn, but I doubt it!

Why Is It That Nobody Ever Says "I Really Built Myself Up Today?"
Tyranny of Shoulds

"I should feel better about me, have a higher self-esteem, selfregard, higher standards, look better, feel better, be grateful, be appreciative, be humble, be sexy, be more up, or not be so down, and, always be at least five pounds lighter or heavier than whatever my weight is."

The founder of Rational Emotive Behavioral Therapy, Dr. Albert Ellis, coined the words "shoulding" and "musterbating." According to Dr. Ellis, the three main musts of musterbating are:

1. I must do well or I'm no good.
2. You must treat me well or you're worthless and deserve to roast in hell.
3. The world must give me exactly what I want, precisely what I want, or it's a horrible, awful place!

When we think we *"should"* be acting a certain "ideal" way, we create a judging and fault-finding inner critic. As a result, a part of us pressures ourselves to follow these rules and feels guilty and bad when we don't.

So here are some common examples of how you "Should Yourself."

"You should care more."

"You should care less."

"You shouldn't care at all."

"You should know by now!"

"You should've gotten up early!"

"You should've worked longer!"

"I should be more successful than I am."

"You shouldn't have eaten that ice cream."

"You should've gone."

"You should've stayed."

"You should've slept longer, less, or not at all."

Ending with "you just never learn!"

Sound familiar?

Here are examples of a favorite variation on "shoulding yourself" known as "the toos."

"Your dream is too much."

"Your ideas are too unrealistic."

"You're too sick."

"You're too fat."

"You're too skinny."

"You're too young."

"You're too old."

"It's too late."

"It's too early."

"You think too much of yourself."

Oh, they are all lies!

Betrayal of Self-Accusations

Self-accusations are another way we beat ourselves up. Here are some examples.

"You're not enough!"

"You're stupid!"

"Nobody likes you!"

"You might as well die!"

"You really loused that up!"

"It's all your fault, you -------- (favorite insult)!"

"See, it's like your father always said!"

"See, it's like your mother always said!"

"See, it's like your girlfriend/boyfriend always said!"

"See, it's like your teacher always said!"

"See it's like your cousin always said!"

"See, it's like your barber always said!"

"See, it's like your doctor always said!"

"See, it's like your plumber always said!"

By changing the way, you talk to yourself, your relationships with everyone else will improve!

Chapter 2 Summary

1. You "should" yourself.
2. It feels like home.
3. You are a mustabator.
4. Self-accusations are another way we beat ourselves up.

5. All beating yourself up is a lie.
6. The antidote is replacing the bad with the good.
7. The truth is the good in you.
8. When you change the way you talk to yourself, your relationships with everyone else will improve.

Chapter 3

Your Shame Committee (And How It Began)

We Were Shamed by Our Parents, and Now We Shame Ourselves

Shame (shām) definition: A painful emotion caused by the belief that one is, or is perceived by others, to be inferior or unworthy of affection or respect because of one's actions, thoughts, circumstances, or experiences.

When you were a kid, you thought the world revolved around you. What occurred in your home communicated to you negative messages about your self-worth. You then internalized these negative messages, and they created shame in you. So, if you had parents that were quick to criticize and slow to say "I'm so proud of you and good job," as most of us did, the seeds of "should," "must," and "shame," were planted in you. Shaming probably goes back many generations in your family, like it does in my family. Shaming like "shoulding," is an intergenerational family tradition!

As a very simple example, most boys were told not to cry. Crying was not considered appropriate behavior for you after the age of seven, or earlier! That was also probably true for your father, his father, and his father's father. Remember this? "Why are you crying? I'll give you something to cry about!"

You also can't forget anger - a forbidden emotion. Your consequences being: "Go to your room, no dinner for you!" "Hand over those Skittles!" "You're grounded!" You could've also been shamed for being too sad, too happy, too distant, or too close, and helping too much with chores or not helping enough with chores.

Fear is another favorite forbidden emotion. Do you remember being called a sissy because you were scared? Maybe you remember your parents shaking their heads and saying, "We just don't get it – there is nothing to fear!" This disapproval of fear causes shame for having the fear and also causes fear of having fear, which causes an escalation of the original fear!

Maybe your family had a very high standard of either scholastic, athletic, or religious behavioral standards. Many families set these expectations so high that they left you feeling "less than enough" if you didn't "hit it out of the ball park." So, beating yourself up became a daily experience.

Most families have their own un-sane cultures.

The Committee

Sometimes there actually seems to be different negative voices in your head. Many people refer to them as "the committee."

The rule of thumb is the worse your childhood, the harsher your committee is; the better your childhood, the "less harsh" your committee is. However, most of us have a "committee" that is ever ready to put us down, lie to us, tell us we are no darn good and generally make our lives a lot harder and unpleasant. Here's an example of what I'm referring to: Let's say you want to get into show business as an actor or a singer. Below are thoughts that you may have depending on your childhood.

Average Childhood: *"You can't sing or act, and even if you do, people will be too polite to tell you what they really think. So, don't embarrass yourself and blow off the audition. I'm just telling you this for your own benefit."*

Bad Childhood: *"You sing or act? Ha, You're a fu---n looser. It's amazing you can walk and chew gum at the same time! Listen moron, you think the world needs another no-talent flunky in show business. Besides, it's like Dad said, you ain't got no talent!"*

See the difference? The type of beating ourselves up when we had an average childhood is comparatively mild, but still strong enough to stop the process and, as you can see, the bad childhood rant is *far more insulting and severe.* The one thing these examples have in common is that without *replacing them with something good,* they can, and usually will, totally stop the acting dream in its tracks.

We've talked about shame, shoulding ourselves, and musterbating, so here is a list of bad childhood experiences that will help you know how you got this way.

Top Ten List of Bad Childhood Experiences

Please read through this list and check all of these childhood experiences that apply to you.

I was shamed by family, teachers, relatives, neighbors or "friends."

I had a distant mother, also known as Ice Queen, Mrs.

Shamer and Blamer, or The Rageaholic.

I had a distant father, also known as Ice King, Mr.

Shamer and Blamer, or The Rageaholic.

I was continually criticized. (Usually including a lot of yelling!)

I was emotionally or physically abandoned by one or both of my parents, whether they were present or not. (This experience for you may have been actually worse if they were present!)

I was over-controlled or smothered.

I was emotionally abused (shamed and/or ignored – seen, but not heard).

I was physically abused.

I was sexually abused.

I was a surrogate parent (i.e. asked to take on the responsibilities of the parent).

If you've had any of these experiences, as I have, you deserve an award for not giving up on life, or on you!! I'm sure there are some bad experiences I left out, so why don't you fill in your experiences and *share it with a trusted friend.*

_____

_____

_____

_____

And if this abuse and neglect wasn't bad enough, *we felt it was "all our fault!"* **This was not true!** See, kids are egocentric, meaning, when you were young you thought "it was all about you," be it good or bad.

As an adult, you have internalized these unhealthy situations which created the lies (always negative) you tell yourself. What once started in your psyche many years ago in childhood as a protection from the scary unknown has become a pattern of continual self-condemnation.

This shapes your idea of who you think you are. Amazingly, it's the rudder of the life you are living now. [1]

It's important that you begin to understand and feel that this abuse and neglect was not your fault!

Chapter 3 Summary

- We were shamed by our parents and others, and now we shame ourselves.

- The worse your childhood, the harsher your committee is

- Most of us have a shaming committee in our head; the better your childhood, the "less harsh" your committee is.

- We felt the abuse and neglect we experienced growing up was "all our fault;" it's important that we begin to understand and feel that this is not true!

---

[1] If anything in this book brings up a lot of fear, anger or other feelings that are impacting your life, it is important that you get support from a counselor or therapist. Please share this book with this person and continue working through it.

Chapter 4

I Suck Radio

It's different for different people. The worse your childhood was, the worse will be the content of this "radio channel."

It's amazing that we all have a library of lousy things people have said to us since we were even as young as four. You have the ability to recall the exact put down, insult, or dismissive comment even if it was said forty or even fifty years ago! You actually maintain a library of these "audio files" to be played the next time you're afraid, triggered, get rejected, think of taking on a new risk or, sometimes, seemingly for no reason at all. It could be your mother's voice: "Why can't you do anything right and be more like your brother?" It could also be your father's voice: "You're just a lazy good-for-nothing!" Maybe you remember a grammar school teacher's voice saying: "You're just a C student!" Also, did you ever have a gym teacher say that you throw like a wimp?"

Examples of Toxic Voices from the Past

Here are some other examples of toxic voices from the past that you may have chosen to remember and replay in your mind over and over again. Please read through this list and check all of these that apply to you.

"You are not doing it right, because you're not doing it the way I asked you to do it!"

"You are low rent!"

"You're just a loser!"

"You'll always be a failure!"

"You're nothing!"

"Hey, know who you are? Mr. Nobody!"

"Your birth was a mistake. You've never been wanted!"

"Pal, you just don't cut it!"

"You've never made the grade!"

"Your mind is like a sieve!"

"You're an airhead!"

"You're too sensitive!"

"Why are you feeling down? I'm working two jobs, and all you have to do is go to school and study!"

"You are so awkward!

"You're a sissy!"

"You're lazy!"

You can fill in additional toxic voices from your childhood below.

_____

_____

_____

_____

Ok, so now circle your top five "toxic recordings" that you keep at the ready, and again, *it's very important that you share your list with a friend you trust!!!*

We all have many of these recordings in our minds, and in a perverse way, we're protective of them as if they were original masters of the Beatles' Abby Road Album.

Congratulations! I bet you feel better now! People are always amazed that people in their lives (or at least in the workshops that I facilitate) are just as cruel to themselves as they are! It's really the worst information that we hear daily, and the insane part of this is that it's all coming from ourselves! We put up with saying terrible things to ourselves that we would never put up with from any relationship.

It's almost like a global radio channel that's on in many of us all the time: It's simply "I suck Radio 24/7!"

It Starts in the Morning

Sometimes the biggest attack we get is when we open our eyes in the morning.

You might hear voices like:

"Hey, look who just got up!" You're guilty! "The failure has just woken up!"

Why Do We Keep Tuning into Toxic Radio?

Remember, you can do absolutely nothing wrong, make no mistakes, and still beat yourself up on a daily basis. Again, the origins of beating ourselves up were created in moments of fear and were ironically created to protect us, which might've made sense at the time, but they sure aren't helping us now! It can be its own numbing experience.

We don't feel joy, happiness and sadness when we're beating

ourselves up. In a strange way, we're in control of the pain and actually are reluctant to stop it. Why? We do it because we've done it for many years! In fact, it is well known that the first five years of a child's life are the most formative years. So, whatever your age is, subtract about five years and that's how long it's probably been going on.

One thing about the mind is that once it creates a pattern of thought it usually repeats it over and over again! For some of us, we're so used to beating ourselves up that most of the time we don't even acknowledge that it's actually happening.

I know this might sound bizarre, but for many of us, but we are actually afraid of letting go of beating ourselves up! We have done it to ourselves for so long that we don't know how we can get along without it. In Chapter 4 we'll begin to talk about how you can let it go!

Chapter 4 Summary

- All of us have a library of lousy things people have said to us since we were even as young as four. This is I Suck Radio, and it's programing in our heads.

- Sometimes the biggest I Suck Radio attack we get is when we open our eyes in the morning.

- Many of us are actually afraid of letting go of the I Suck Radio channel in our minds. We have done it to ourselves for so long that we don't know how we can get along without it.

Chapter 5

A Spiritual Solution – Are You Kidding Me?

Thought-Based Solutions

When you Google "Beating Yourself Up," you will find hundreds of articles and blogs about selfabuse - being toxically self-critical, and the only so-

lutions that are usually suggested are thought-based. Here's an example:

"A good way to stop thinking negatively is to consciously identify your negative thoughts, and then actively replace negative thinking with realistic thinking or self-soothing thoughts by reminding yourself that 'Everything is going to be OK' or 'I can do this' or 'I can get through this.'"

Here is another example of a thought-based solution:

"When you feel you're about to beat yourself up, ask yourself these two questions: What lesson can I learn here? What will I do differently next time?"

Try using those thought-based techniques when you just got

Build Yourself Up Without Limits

fired; you're about to make a speech; you didn't get a text back from your boyfriend or girlfriend, and it's been more than a day; you are alone again on a Saturday night; you got written out of the will; your car was towed away; you just got an eviction notice; you botched a sale; or you received a whopper of a tax bill. These techniques are as helpful as trying to lasso a run-away bull on a golf course with dental floss!

Affirmations are one kind of thought-based solution. Affirmations are states of being or goals that you say to yourself as if you have already achieved that state of being or goal – but you have not yet done so.

Here are some examples:

1. I am calm despite the fact that my husband (or wife) just left me, and I have no money to pay the mortgage that is due in one week.
2. I feel love toward my boss, even though he fired me yesterday.
3. I welcome challenges - even an eviction notice.
4. I am happy and joyous throughout the day, even though they just towed my car away.

See how effective these affirmations are when your anger or anxiety feels like it is an 11 out of 10!

What events have sent you over-the-edge lately? List here the lousy things you said to yourself during those events and list any thought-based solutions (including affirmations), you tried.

Event:

Thought-based Solutions I Said to Me:

Lousy Things I Said to Me:

_____

Thought-based Solutions I Said to Me:

_____

Event:

_____

Lousy Things I Said to Me:

_____

Thought-based Solutions I Said to Me:

_____

Event:

_____

Lousy Things I Said to Me:

_____

Thought-based Solutions I Said to Me:

_____

Did any of this improve anything for you? Or did it make matters worse? Now share these with a trusted friend and ask them about their experiences.

For how many people do thought-based solutions work? For most people in my workshops, the quick answer is *none*. Maybe when you're reading about them, you get a hopeful feeling, but it doesn't last very long.

Thought-based solutions do not work for most people, because shoulding on ourselves and beating ourselves up is caused by negative emotional energy in us that has been around for most of our lives, and we cannot solve an emotional problem with a thought-based solution.

The Solution Is Spiritual

Even though you've never thought of it this way, beating yourself up is actually an addiction! Many recovery programs that have been around for decades have proven one thing: To stop compulsive behavior a spiritual solution is required.

You're probably saying at this point, what is a spiritual solution, and what the heck does it have to do with my emotional condition, and where does one end and the other begin?

What is the Spiritual Condition?

OK, let's start with the word "Spiritual." Getting into definitions of the word that probably cause more confusion than anything else:

The English Oxford Living Online Dictionary defines "Spiritual" as:

"Relating to or affecting the human spirit or soul as opposed to material or physical things."

Merriam Webster's Online Dictionary defines "Spiritual" in even more confusing terminology:

"1. Of, relating to, consisting of, or affecting the spirit: incorporeal <e.g. spiritual needs> a: of or relating to sacred matters <e.g. spiritual songs> b: ecclesiastical rather than lay or temporal <e.g. spiritual authority> <e.g. lords' spiritual> concerned with religious values."

Perhaps the word "Spiritual" gives you a warm fuzzy feeling, or perhaps it makes you sick to your stomach, or even irritates the heck out of you!

I know "Spiritual" may bring up uncomfortable images. Perhaps the images that come to your mind are from a church, a synagogue, or a mosque, which can call-up for you painful experiences, as they do for me. Or maybe you are squirming while thinking of the scent of sandalwood incense wafting through the air, and wind chimes tinkling in the distance and people chanting away!

I suggest you open your mind to the realty that there is a positive energy in all of us! The source of this spiritual energy in us is a force that is much more powerful, intelligent, and good than you think. This positive energy is what allowed Thomas Edison to discover electricity, and that same brilliant creative energy created you too! The word "Spiritual" is basically a description of a part of you that is very bright, creative, strong, and aligned with a force for the good in the universe.

This spiritual energy is not something to be scoffed at or feared, but rather to be seen as an anchor and a source that will help you solve your problems, including beating yourself up, shoulding on yourself and musterbating!

What is the Emotional Condition?

Ok, now that we have "Spiritual" squared away, so what's with this term "Emotional Condition?"

Well, McGraw-Hill defines "Emotion" as:

"A mood, affect or feeling of any kind – e.g, anger, excitement, fear, grief, joy, hatred, love." [2]

OK. It looks like this definition is fairly easy to relate to and

---

[2] McGraw-Hill Concise Dictionary of Modern Medicine. © 2002 by The McGraw-Hill Companies, Inc. (Quoted from TheFreeDictionary.com).

understand. Emotions are basically our feelings or our mood.

The Flow Between the Emotional and Spiritual Conditions

So, does our spiritual condition affect our emotional condition? Or is it the other way around? Well, what I've found is that there is no boundary between the two. One flows into the other effortlessly, changing within you throughout the day. We may have fear spikes during the day that can cause us to make bad choices if we are in poor spiritual condition.

However, when we are in good spiritual condition, we can quell the emotional spikes and then make good choices. I have coached many people over the years, and *all of these people* report that they feel, think and act very differently when they are in good spiritual condition -- they make much better choices, and what is life but a succession of choices?

Chapter 5 Summary

- Thought-based solutions do not work for most people, because shoulding on ourselves and beating ourselves up is caused by negative emotional energy in us, and we cannot solve an emotional problem with a thought-based solution.

- Beating ourselves up is actually an addiction, and to stop compulsive behavior a spiritual solution is required.

- "Spiritual" is basically a description of a part of you that is very bright, creative, strong, and aligned with a force for the good in the universe.

- Spiritual energy is to be seen as an anchor and a source that will help you solve your problems, including beating yourself up, shoulding on yourself and musterbating!

- There is an inter-play between the emotional and spiritual parts of us. One flows into the other effortlessly, changing within us throughout the day.

- We may have fear spikes during the day that can cause us to make bad choices if we are in poor spiritual condition. However, when we are in good spiritual condition, we can quell them and make good choices.

Chapter 6

Museum States ™

"Museum States ™" Are Micro-Addictions, and They Feel Like Home o, *it's not about walking around your local museum feverishly obsessing about Van Gogh's painting "The Starry Night" or spending hours analyzing a Henry Moore sculpture of a bull. "Museum States ™" are the emotional patterns of your present life that are dysfunctional and unpleasant, but they do feel like "home" and, therefore, you will seek them out again and again and, of course, never know you're doing that. See, you spent the first 17 to 18 years of your life experiencing these states over and over again. In short, you lived with what you decided was reality and have been the protective "curator" of these Museum States. ™ The word "curator" means a person who is in charge of a museum's exhibit, or the entire museum.*

We all have different childhoods and come from many different cultures, but there are basic patterns we actually seek out no matter what is our culture. As I mentioned, the reason why you are "seeking out these unhealthy states" is that they feel like home. Home, being the way, you felt most of the time when you were growing up. These patterns have been alive in you for so many years that they have become unconscious reflexes. In short, they are micro-addictions.

For example, as a child, if you constantly felt you were "striking out" or "not hitting the mark," you can be addicted to *feeling less than enough.* Why? This feels like home!

If you struggled for positive acknowledgement, love, and even fun, as I did, you most probably are seeking out again and again and are addicted *to the state of "struggle"* because you believe that struggle is "normal." Given my past, I pushed away ease and sought out struggle for years. I didn't know why! I thought to continually struggle was the way life was meant to be. When I realized I was wrong about that belief, I was very uncomfortable because it meant I had to leave the familiarity of this ancient belief or "home." I didn't want to admit that it felt like home for me, but it did!

If you had parents that were ill, or addicted, you might have become the parent of your parents, or sisters and brothers. Then, as an adult, feeling compelled to take care of others and not yourself is another micro-addictive state that you will seek out again and again. Why? You know the answer... It feels like home!

None of these choices seem logical, do they? Of course not! It has nothing to do with logic. It has to do with living with your family for 17 or 18 years and deciding these states *were reality for you and so they have become unconscious reflexes.*

"Museum States" ™ Are Mind Apps

There are mobile apps that are "doors" to utilizing a service. Museum States ™ have a similar function and, therefore, I call them "Mind Apps." The name of each Museum State ™ has two to four words, but these words open "the door" to a world of these very old emotional patterns. The better your childhood, the milder the Museum States ™ will be. The worse your childhood was, the more insane they will be. Museum states are Mind Apps that govern the work we choose, the way we work, and who we choose to love!

When you think of living in a family from birth to eighteen years -- that is an incredibly long period of time to develop patterns of living that "feel like home," so no matter how bad they are, we don't want to leave them. If you do work that makes you unhappy, stressed, demeaned, and yet you keep returning to it, and can't figure out why, it's probably because the acceptance of that work comes out of the core of two or three of your Museum States™.

For example, it's like the guy who grows up in a home with a bully of a father and chooses to be a rodeo clown. Most of the time he's being chased around the ring by a 1,700-pound bull, and he says "Hey man – I don't know why I'm in this crazy job!" This guy has the Mr. Guilty and the Superhuman Museum States™, and he has them to the max!!!

The description of each Museum State ™ that follows is in no way intended to provide a comprehensive analysis of why each state exists in you, or its evolution in your life. The short description is just meant to "jog an association" of your familiarity with it. Museum States ™ are emotional patterns that we had *unconsciously* every day - that is, until now! You may, or not, identify with all of them, but *you definitely will identify with some of them!* You will know exactly which Museum States ™ are yours. Why? Well, they feel like home!

When I describe and explain Museum States ™ to my clients, they usually have two reactions. Their first reaction is relief as they know what Museum States ™ they have. Why? Well, they've been having them for decades, so it's no surprise to them; they're tickled that somebody has put a name to their madness.

The second reaction my clients often have is discomfort, as they are getting the idea that I'm suggesting that they let these states go since they are not doing them any good. There would oftentimes be a tone of reluctance in their voices and lack of eagerness in their faces. This is totally understandable because I'm telling them that it's safe to leave home, but they're not totally convinced. At this stage, I would tell them this joke:

"I walk over to a guy who is sitting on a park bench, and he is clearly upset. I say to him 'What's wrong?' He says to me: 'My wife hits me over the head with a frying pan every morning when I come down to breakfast!' I say 'Man, why don't you leave home???' He tells me: 'Hey, I love the eggs!!!'

This joke has helped my clients to see that any benefit that they would be getting from their Museum States is overshadowed by the detrimental effects. Anyway, it's OK to start off with some reluctance. All I'm suggesting at this point is that you look at these different Museum States ™ and see if any of them fit you. So relax, and let's go ahead and take a tour of the Museum States™, some of which will be yours.

MUSEUM STATES ™ EXHIBIT LISTING

Crumbaholic ™ Edge-Meister™ Control Freak ™ Mr. or Ms. Guilty Perfectionist ™ Snobaholic ™ Nitpicker™ Panicker ™ Struggleaholic ™ Misery-Maven ™ Crises Queen or King ™ The LessThaner ™ The Worrier ™ The Rageaholic ™

The Gloom and Doomer ™ The Superhuman ™ The Eggshell Walker ™ Angst-glutton ™ The Pleaser ™

The Crumbaholic ™

This is a Museum State ™ where you feel comfortable with seeking out the "crumbs of life:" Crumbs of money, love, joy, and happiness. Your bucket list is more like a beach pail list. So, for example, being a Crumbaholic ™ causes you to put up with a spouse, boyfriend or girlfriend who cheats on you or abuses you. Or maybe you are in a work situation and are getting paid far below what you are worth. You're actually *uncomfortable* with "the whole loaf" of "all good things." Why? As a kid you had to work triple time to get crumbs of love, fun, joy, and even peace. Your parents believed in criticism of you as "your daily bread" and building you up with love and support as "cake" that may be given to you once or twice a year.

P.S. They didn't get anything better from their parents!

Edge-Meister ™

If this is your Museum State ™, you are addicted to "living on the edge" regarding finances, work, love and time. You continually create and recreate work and business situations that cause you to live on the financial edge *again and again,* and you wonder why? Financial comfort just isn't comfortable for you! You don't have much in the way of savings and insurance, and let's not talk about your "status" with the IRS! If you don't have that old anxiety in the pit of your stomach, you don't feel alive, do you? You view the word "comfort" with the same suspicion you use when looking at the ingredients on a package of supermarket hot dogs!

Now let's look at how you deal with time. You often experience the glare of your boss when you show up to work meetings ten minutes late, and your significant other is threatening insignificance because she's tired of you being two hours late to dinner and reheating for the third time the Chinese food she cooked from scratch!

The Control Freak ™

Yes, I know that your wanting to control everything has to do with your feeling safe. Maybe you grew up in a tightly controlled environment, where you were so overscheduled as a child that you had to put "climbing a tree" in your day planner! So you now only feel comfortable with a lot of control. Or perhaps your childhood home was a tornado swirling around you, and you felt out of control. Being a control freak allows you now to feel protected. The problem is that even your cat is asking if its "meow" is OK! And your kid is already in rehab, and he's only six years old! Anyway, you're starting to understand that this has got to stop, but how? Keep working through this book!

Mr. or Ms. Guilty

If Mr. or Ms. Guilty is one of your Museum States ™, you have a full-time prosecutor voice in your head which evolved in the first 17 to 18 years of your life where you were blamed or shamed by your family on a weekly, if not daily basis. You had the type of childhood where you were yelled at or hit before your babysitter arrived, just in case you were to do something wrong when your parents were away. If your sister had cramps, your dad had ulcers, your mother got fat, or your dog buried your grandmother's earing in the backyard, it was all your fault!

You were bullied by your parent, grandparent or older brother or sister and told that you were responsible for all of the problems in the family, and at some point, you bought into this lie. "It's all your fault!" "Can't you do anything right?" "You screwed up again!" are thoughts that often go through your mind. You allow people to "should" and blame you and take it all in, when there is no need for you to do so! If you walked into a courtroom you'd be tempted to say "Your honor, whatever it is, I'm guilty!"

The Perfectionist ™

Being a Perfectionist is a common Museum State ™ for millions of people. Demanding perfection in yourself and others is wellordered madness!

You had crazy parents that gave you "unconditional love" on the condition of a straight-A report card! Now, you've done it to your kids. Your son has internalized your perfectionism and has fine-tuned it so he's now pissed off because he only got an A in his AP College courses, and he only made Junior Varsity on the high school football team! He doesn't have enough time to sleep with all of his schoolwork, team practices and partying. Your daughter even has performance anxiety when playing with Legos! You're starting to see that your perfectionism can have unhealthy consequences.

The Snobaholic ™

Snobs come in many forms and colors. You take refuge in feeling superior towards people outside of your wonderful social circle of exaltedness. You may be the person who only will have friends who earn in the 6-digit figures and have had at least one face-lift this year! You express your superiority with body language and words or by acting as if others don't exist. You think that your way is the right way, and therefore it's the only way. If someone has a different approach, then you simply freeze them out. It's my way or the highway!

People outside of your circle are often angry at you. You are surprised by this, because you didn't think that they had the intelligence to see your disdain for them. I get it! When you were in Little League your father may never have come to see you at bat. He was always too busy working on his tan at the yacht club! You have a disease – it's called the "looking good disease," and there is a cure, and you are reading it!

The Nitpicker

Nothing is up to par for you if you have the Nitpicker Museum State. ™ If you were on a beautiful island overlooking the sea with gourmet cuisine, you'd find fault with the soufflé – it's just not high enough! And the sun would just be too bright! And you'd criticize the waiter for being too helpful! No one is exempt from your nitpicking, not even you!

Well, you've come by it naturally, as your dad would constantly criticize your crayon drawings that your mom scotch-taped to the refrigerator. In fact, if you can't find something wrong with something, you just don't feel right, do you? Well, remember, your dad comes from a long line of nitpickers!

Anyway, you are starting to understand that this has got to stop, but how? Keep working through this book and stop nitpicking yourself and others!

Angst-glutton ™

If you have the Angst-glutton Museum State, you have a lowgrade continual anxiety and unease that unfortunately feels like normal, at least to you! It also feels like a low level of stress that is non-stop.

Yes, it started in you when you were very young, and it was caused by continued uncertainty. It was about whether the knock on the door was the pizza delivery guy or the landlord asking about why the rent was late again! Stability was missing in your childhood experience. It was there sometimes, and sometimes not. It got so bad that you had angst over the Roadrunner being chased by Wile E. Coyote, even though the Roadrunner was never caught!

The Panicker

The Panicker Museum State™ is similar to the Angst Glutton, only it's ramped up 150%! So, if one of your Museum States ™ is being a Panicker, tranquility is just not in your vocabulary! If someone says "take it easy," you don't know what the heck they are talking about! Excessive stress and anxiety is like a highspeed acid running through your system.

It could've been caused by your dad who practiced "Wipe Out" on the drums at three in the morning and criticized you for not being able to sleep through it! Or perhaps your parents didn't think your opinion was worth anything, and you had a mother or father who broadcasted their opinions and ordered you around. They said they loved you until you said how you really felt. Then they sent you to the dog house!!

Stick around and keep reading and you'll see that there is an antidote for this Museum State™ as well as the other Museum States™ I have discussed.

Struggleaholic ™

"Take the elevator? That's for wimps!

It doesn't feel right unless it's hard! Being a Struggleaholic ™ is one of my own top five personal Museum States™. It came from my experience of working very hard as a child for love, praise, fun and joy. So many things I've done had to have a struggle component to them, or there would be a voice in my head that would say "easy - that's no fun!" So, I wouldn't do things that were easy and fun, or I would make them hard and filled with struggle. I would be involved in simple situations, and I would work hard to make them complicated!

The Misery-Maven ™

If you feel miserable much of the time, you have the Misery-Maven Museum State™. It's not about seeing the glass as half-full or half-empty, you just don't see any water in the glass at all! Your internal view of the world is filtered through a gray lens.

If this is how you felt growing up most of the time, you will seek out situations that make you miserable in the blink of an eye! For example, if you had to sleep in a bed under a leaky pipe when you were growing up, you would most likely seek out realty that feels like a leaky pipe!

The Crises King or Queen ™

Peace and order are no favorites of yours. You are addicted to taking normal situations and making them insane. Hey, it's no wonder, as you moved fifty times as a kid - that is, when your daddy wasn't locked up for some child support issue from his first, or was it his second marriage? Mom was always under a haze of cigarette smoke, with a permanent snarl on her upper lip. She was waiting for the welfare check to arrive, so she could spent it on lotto, beef jerky and enough booze to give her a buzz that would take her right into tomorrow!

The LessThaner ™

If you walk around feeling less than enough, then you're *seeking* out the state of being a "LessThaner" as one of your Museum States ™. This is usually caused because you felt for many years that you didn't live up to your parents' expectations, which were basically impossible for anyone to live up to. Even them! Hey, it could've been anything from not getting straight A's, to not being "religious" enough, to not making the Little League line-up. Or come to think of it, maybe it was not winning the biggest tomato award at your local 4 H club fair!

The Worrier ™

Worry is a negative dream based on fear. It is not reality! It is the voice in our heads that creates an endless parade of "What Ifs." What if it doesn't work out? What if the relationship dies? What if I can't raise the funds? What If I fail? These are all examples of "What Ifs" that may go through the Worrier's mind. When we really look closely at worry, it is self-indulgent. When we worry, we are indulging ourselves in an unhealthy negative dream, rather than building ourselves up by focusing on positive outcomes.

This ancient condition is caused by a childhood filled with uncertainty of finances, love and family members "acting out." For example, Uncle Leo would sometimes show up in his Indian costume at your birthday party and chase you around the room with a rubber tomahawk, while dad was under the dining room table in an alcoholic blackout!

The Rageaholic ™

If you have the Rageaholic Museum State, you constantly feel that you need to explode at people in order to get attention. Your parents never understood your anger stemmed from fear. Neither did you. However, tantrums proved for you to be an effective emotional device that helped you get what you wanted. It has helped you get what you want in the past, but now it's ripping up your life. You are on your third marriage, and your husband said he was working late at the office, which you noticed was closed as you drove by. You're ready to "let him have it again!" You punished your kid and told him that he couldn't have dessert for a year. You suspect that he planted the banana peel in the kitchen that caused you to fall face down in the cat's water dish! Now the cat's pissed off too!

The Pleaser ™

Growing up you decided that to survive and to be loved, you had to give your family, friends, coaches and teachers what they wanted -- regardless of what that cost you! For a while it worked. The problem is that people-pleasing now leaves you feeling resentful, tired and used.

As a child you may have grown up being "The Actor" – you know how to be different people for different people – in order to handle these demands. The question is *where do you begin and end?* You have so many acts you do with so many people that it's hard for you to keep them straight. The one thing you don't know is that all you have to be is you, and that's enough!

The Gloom and Doomer ™

The Gloom and Doomer™ is a state of being afraid of "what's around the corner." If you came home from school every day and didn't know whether you were going to find Dr. Jekyll or Mr. Hyde, you experienced terror spikes. This state is also about making small difficulties into huge problems. If your parents had no problem-solving skills and they freaked-out with each problem they encountered, you are likely to have this Museum State ™. Remember the time when your cat knocked over the fondue, which spilled on the white shag carpeting, and your Mom melted down at the same pace as the cheese? Your cousins are still talking about it!

The Superhuman ™

If you had sick or alcoholic parents, and especially if you were the oldest of your brothers and sisters, this can easily be your Museum State. ™ If something goes wrong, you blame yourself, put yourself down, and are very reluctant to congratulate yourself for anything. You blame yourself for everything because you feel responsible for everything. The last person you take care of is *you*. If you were on an airplane, you would hand an oxygen mask over to the guy sitting in the seat next to you, even as you were turning a light shade of blue! You take pride in your lack of self-care that you inwardly refer to as "selfless" while, at the same time, you resent the heck out of *those selfish jerks that never appreciate you!*

The Eggshell Walker ™

"Did I make too much noise breathing? Sorry!"

Living at home for you was an emotional minefield with each entry into a room, especially if Mom and Dad were having one of their freak-outs, battles or just stony silences. You never knew what was going to set them off, so you did everything in your power to be quiet. Now you seek out loud and obnoxious people who cause you to experientially "walk on eggshells", which feels to you like "home." ™

How Museum States™ Apply to Your Own Life

All Museum States ™ create suffering! All Museum States ™ are micro-addictions!

So now it would be a good idea for you to list the Museum States ™ that you saw here in this book that you personally identify with, and list others that I did not mention in this book:

My personal Museum States ™ are:

1. _____
2. _____
3. _____
4. _____
5. _____
6. _____
7. _____
8. _____
9. _____
10. _____
11. _____
12. _____

Now share your Museum States™ list with a friend or friends you trust and ask them about theirs.

It's common for people to have many of these Museum States ™, so don't freak out if you've listed a lot of them! It's important that you accept them and begin to have a sense of humor about them. That is the first step to changing their role in your life.

Our Museum States ™ are very much like showing up at the track right before the race, and saying *"wait, I have to put ten pounds on each leg!"*

Here are examples of what people will say to you about some of your Museum States ™. Remember, all they can see is your behavior.

- "Why do you ask for so little in life?"
- "You're a stress junky. Aren't you?" "You love it!"
- "Dude - It's like you're addicted to being pissed off!"
- "OMG - Your sales division came in last. It's not your fault, but you're taking all the blame."

- "Babe, you are such a 'kiss-ass' pleaser, aren't you?"
- "Every time we have a board meeting, you never speak up - you look like you're in front of a firing squad!"

These accusatory comments are usually followed by the equally accusatory: "What's wrong with you?" This is often followed by the classic: "What were you thinking?" Of course, both of these statements mean the same thing, which is that the person is judging you negatively and most likely you weren't thinking at all. You were just in "an old Museum State" ™ that felt like home...."

Ok, now write about how your Museum States ™ are affecting your life now.

Your Work:

_____

_____

_____

_____

_____

_____

_____

Share with others you trust!!!

Your Love Life:

_____

_____

_____

_____

Share with others you trust!!!

Your Friends and Family.

Share with others you trust!!!

Your Art:

Share with others you trust!!!

Here is an advanced exercise you may want to try – either by yourself, with your buddies or in one of my workshops. Review the dialogue in the Worrier section below, as an example. Then write down an internal or external conversation that you recently had that is coming from one of your Museum States ™.

Megan: Why is he so late on our date night? What if he's out with his cute assistant . . . she's so smart too!

Mike: Hi Megan. I'm really sorry! I know I am calling you an hour after I was supposed to see you. I had to keep my focus on my business deal. I have great news for you - I just closed the largest deal of my career!

Megan: You know I was worried sick. You didn't respond to my text messages!

Mike: For God's sake – I just closed the biggest deal of my life and you can't think beyond yourself and your worry! How many times has this happened where I have told you that I can't return a text, because I am in the middle of a large deal, and I can't have my concentration broken! Why can't you just assume that if we have a date on a Friday night, that it may get delayed because I am in the middle of a deal?

Megan: Well, I just don't understand why you can't take 30 seconds to text me so I don't worry!

Mike: Megan!!! This is unbelievable! You know what? I'm just not in the mood tonight! Talk to you tomorrow! Bye.

Then go ahead and act out our sketch with your buddies or workshop partners. As an alternative, you may prefer to skip the writing and just do interactive improvisation of your Museum State

™ with your buddies or in one of my workshops.

As I discussed at the beginning of this chapter, the word "curator" means a person who is in charge of a museum's exhibit, or the entire museum. Likewise, we're the protective curators of our Museum States ™. Regardless of how much suffering they have caused us, just like a real curator of a museum, we are protective of them! Why not? They feel like our home! Aren't people protective of their homes? Well, that applies to us as well!

Before I did the work to leave my Museum States ™, I was:

A connoisseur of crumbs!

A valedictorian of misery!

A Phi Beta Kappa of stress!

A Magna Cum Laude of struggle!

A graduate student of gloom!

And I ended up writing a doctoral thesis on "less-thanerism™!!!"

This was insanity!!!!! I bet you feel the same way regarding some of your Museum States™!

Remember, all it takes to open the door to our Museum States™ is usually fear. Fear of losing what we have, and fear of not getting what we want. It happens with the speed of a blink! The question is how to not "seek out" these Museum States ™, or how to get out of them quickly!

At this point, you're probably saying, "Enough already about Museum States ™! What's the solution?" We will be discussing that in Chapters 8, 9, and 10.

Chapter 6 Summary

- "Museum States ™" Are Micro-Addictions, and They Feel

Like Home.

- Museum States ™ are the emotional patterns of your present life that are dysfunctional and unpleasant, but they do feel like "home" and, therefore, *you will* seek them out again and again.

- The word "curator" means a person who is in charge of a museum's exhibit, or the entire museum. Likewise, we're the protective curators of our Museum States ™.

- Museum States ™ are mind apps that govern the work we choose, the way we work, and who we choose to love!

- All it takes to open the door to our Museum States™ is usually fear.

- It's common for people to have many Museum States ™.

- We may dislike Museum States™ but we defend them and hold them close and tight

- It's important that you accept your Museum States ™ and begin to have a sense of humor about them. That is the first step to changing their role in your life.

Chapter 7

The Power of Spiritual Energy

"OMG! He's Talking About God!"

Well to start, we're praising ourselves for what we do and giving God most of the credit!

"Oh no, he said God!"

Listen, I totally get it if the God thing doesn't work for you! For a long time it didn't work for me. The wars, dictators, and really bad people getting power, greed for greed's sake, good people suffering, global warming, insane military arms sales, the betrayals by politicians, the abuse and neglect you never deserved, the insanity of your parents, and all the nutty people in your family tree going back many generations make it very hard to believe in God.

But then we see some incredible things happen that demonstrate that there is a powerful, good force in the universe that does ultimately defeat the bad in the world. When people believe in that force, and do the footwork to defeat evil, amazing things have happened. The United States and Allies fought a very difficult two-front war and succeeded in defeating Hitler and Japan. The Jews as a people survived the Holocaust, and the State of Israel was established in 1948. Gandhi led a peaceful, spiritual movement to free India, and India gained independence in 1947. The non-violent civil rights movement changed the shape of race relations in the United States, so that our first Black President, Barak Obama, was elected on November 4, 2008, about 45 years after Martin Luther King delivered his speech "I have a dream" to a massive group of civil rights marchers gathered in Washington DC. These are just a few instances that demonstrate the power of God working through people.

Here's the thing, you have a choice in the way you live every day: It's either living by fear or faith. Fear is what always drives beating yourself up. Faith will build you up, no matter what! So, for the moment, let's let get of the word "God," if that is a problem for you, and let's look at other words. Perhaps on your journey through your life to make big decisions you use for internal guidance words like:

Gut Reaction

Hunch

The One

The Source of the Universe

The Force

Higher Power

Providence

Serendipity

The Still Small Voice Within

The Great Mystery

Use whatever words you would like to name this positive spiritual energy in you and outside of you. I use the word "God" in this book as the name for this spiritual energy, but please substitute in whatever word that resonates with you.

Even with the unfairness of my experience as a child, I have still been able to believe in this spiritual energy. For me this energy is experiential. Words that come to mind for me are peace, serenity, acceptance, kindness, connection, help, and direction.

That's not how I felt growing up.

Here's my story:

My father left our home when he realized he was married to a schizophrenic woman. I was about age two at the time. So, I was raised in a household with a mentally ill mother present, well at least some of the time! She kept going back and forth from our home to the asylum. Due to my mother's and father's absence, I had abandonment issues. But when she came home, her behavior scared the crap out of me! Also, I had a step father who spent most of the week isolated in the basement. One of my uncles, who was cognitively disabled, lived with us, so it was "a real party!" I was raised by my grandmother and grandfather, who took care of my physical needs, but were not there for me emotionally.

If this wasn't bad enough, my grandmother set the bar very high on the religious perfectionism scale. I felt guilty for not being as "religious" as my grandmother would've liked. I was sent to a "religious school" where I was physically hit, and I was told by the "religious teachers" that I was "lazy." I hated going to this school, hated the teachers, and felt less-than enough for not embracing the "religious teachings." So, like Mark Twain, I did believe in God, but at that time the relationship was strained. If it wasn't for my wonderful uncle that I used to visit weekly, I don't know how I would have survived!

At this religious school I was told to fear God as an old man sitting on a throne who watched my every move, just waiting for me to "screw up." Then, there would be some negative mark on my "celestial report card!" I thought that this might restrict the privileges I would enjoy in the afterlife! Maybe I'd have to go on a waiting list for harp lessons, or I wouldn't be given my angel's pilot's license. Gee, maybe I could be grounded in heaven!

If your relationship with God is based on fear or resentment, I understand! That was my old relationship with God. What I learned, and am passing on to you, is that the relationship is really about love and forgiveness, and *God has no part ever in beating us up!* That's been our department....

Using Spiritual Energy to Dial-Back Beating Yourself Up

Again, the way you define and name the powerful, spiritual energy outside of or inside of you in which you've experienced positive occurrences, or the protection from negative occurrences, is up to you. My job is to help you bring this energy into your daily life and to help you "dial-back" beating yourself up.

Harnessing this energy and practicing the tools in this book will do just that even if you:

Just crashed into another car while texting!

Got defriended by everyone on Facebook, including people who were actually your friends!

Got linked Out of LinkedIn!

Forgot to lock the car, and your briefcase was stolen with your speech that you worked on for months that you were planning to give to an investor group in a half-hour!

Drove to the airport, and with only two hours before the flight, you realized in horror that you left your laptop (or luggage) at home!

Failed a test!

Discovered your application for government benefits was denied!

Found out your work proposal was rejected, and the work was given to your competitor!

Were rejected from a relationship, job, rock band, sewing circle, real estate deal, sports team, social circle, bowling club, or a weekly card game!

Left the cake your wife made for her mother's 90th birthday party in the back seat of the car on a 100-degree day.

Checked today's mail and read the bank statement that stated your 401

K is now a "201K!"

Blew your diet for the (be honest) time!

Had one hundred bad internet dates!

My point is that it doesn't matter what we do wrong. We can build ourselves up no matter what! *I mean unconditionally!!!*

Remember, how many hundreds of times you have beaten yourself up when you made meaningless mistakes? It could've been over something small like a broken shoelace or burning the toast. Also, you may have rarely praised or even acknowledged yourself in the successes and breakthroughs of your past.

As you know, "beating yourself up" never takes a day off and loves nothing more than to "bring out the big guns" the next time you screw up. What good has it ever done you?

List here the "great benefits" that you've personally experienced from your many years of beating yourself up!

1. _____

2. _____

3. _____

4. _____

5. _____

Bet you couldn't even list one!

How many projects have you beaten yourself up about? How many businesses, relationships, hobbies, goals, and visions?

God Shots

As I said, as a child, I was raised to fear God and fear. However, in looking back and revaluating my past, I've seen that I was taken care of and loved far more than I thought.

Here's my God Shot story:

When I was in my twenties, I decided it was time to track down my father in Israel, who I had not seen since I was a toddler. After many attempts to locate his address through telephone directory assistance, I kept coming up empty. One day, while looking for work as an entertainment production assistant, I was in an office building in Manhattan where there were many producers' offices, and for some reason, I thought it would be a good idea to put my resume under the doors, as if it were a take-out pizza menu from a nearby restaurant. This was way before the internet!

Well, one of the doors opened and a guy comes out and says: "Mr. Stewart wants to see you." Mr. Stewart was a dance company producer, and after glancing over my meager resume, he asked me if I would drive him from Manhattan to North Carolina and work as a production assistant at the music festival at Duke University in the month of June. The only problem was that I didn't have a driver's license! This, for me, did not present a problem of any consequence. After about fifteen to twenty minutes of driving instruction from my friend David (including five minutes of highway driving at 30 mph), I showed up at the entrance to the Lincoln Tunnel, got into Mr.

Stewart's MercedesBenz, and drove sort of competently from Manhattan to Durham, North Carolina, in slightly under eight hours. The fact that I was not pulled over, did not crash into something, and was able to concentrate on that long of a trip was in itself a miracle. Wait - it gets better!

In the intro session of the music festival that night, I met a Romanian composer named Jan, who had studied in Israel for ten years. I mentioned that I was born in Israel, and we hit it off! The next day, Jan introduced me to Geori, who worked for the Jerusalem Post. I mentioned that my father lived in Israel. He asked me my father's name. I told him it was Eliezer Deutsch. As it turns out, Eliezer Deutsch was not in the Israeli Phone Book because he had changed his last name to Dorot. This guy, Giori, happened to know my father before he changed his last name, and he gave me the phone number of the film studio where my father worked. Giori was probably the only person in the United States who knew that my father had changed his name!

Coming back to Manhattan, I called my father from my girlfriend's apartment, leaving the message, "Hi Dad. This is your son from America. Please give me a call." He called me back, which was an amazing conversation at three in the morning! Three weeks later I was in Israel and was embraced by a father I had not seen in over twenty-seven years. It all happened by putting my resume under the door! These experiences were so incredible that I just knew they were not mere coincidences! Since then, I really have not felt alone on this planet.

Okay, now let's hear your story about how God has helped you. So, turn on the computer, get out the iPad, note pad, journal, loose leaf note-book, or write in this workbook your story about how God, providence, or the universe has saved or helped you. When you finish your story, read it out loud first, and then read it to a trusted friend. It would also be a great idea if your friend wrote their God Shot story and read it to you.

Your God Shot Story:

(Attach More Sheets If You Need to Do So)

How do you feel now? Do you feel somehow more connected, at ease or at peace?

Everything You Do and Have Is More God's Success Than Yours!

Everything you do and have is more God's success than yours! Okay, this might be a little jarring, upsetting, or anger-producing. I totally get that, but let's continue on this journey, and all I ask is that you keep an open mind. So, let's expand on this.

Let me break it down to things you do, have, use, and enjoy, and like everybody else, often totally take for granted. We have many abilities, and each one is a gift to us that could not have been created just by chance – a universal intelligence had to have created these highly complex abilities and talents! So, in fact, our utilizing these talents and abilities is more God's success than ours!

Imagination

Imagination is the creative ability to form images, ideas, and sensations in the mind. Imagination helps you to visualize solutions and in so doing helps you to solve problems. Clearly, this is a gift you were given, and your utilizing this gift is more God's success than yours!

Persistence

Persistence is continuing in a course of action in spite of difficulty or opposition. In short: "to keep on keeping on!" Well, you were born with it, and you have more of it than you think, but like any ability, it gets stronger with practice. It's more God's success than yours!

The Reliability and Functioning of Our Bodies

Ever think about your digestive system's multifaceted processing? No, most of us haven't, but it works automatically 24-7. What about the complex functions of your mind and how they are the control center for managing every aspect of your body? Our bodies are a miracle of reliability and function. They are like very comfortable space crafts that we take for granted. We possess little knowledge as to how they work and even less appreciation of what they do. For example, if I asked you how you sing a high note and then a low note, could you explain it? For that matter, how do you sing at all?

Moving your hand and picking up a spoon -- Hmmm. Well, talk about an activity that we take for granted! Dr. Ari Berkowitz, in a Psychology Today article illustrates the interrelationship between our brain and basic physical hand movement.

"The idea is that nerve cells (neurons) in certain parts of the brain, such as the motor cortex, normally generate electrical signals (or spikes) that trigger particular movements. Different neurons trigger different movements. A particular sequence of brain neuron spikes causes a precise movement sequence such as we use to grasp and manipulate an object. These brain neurons normally activate neurons in the spinal cord, which in turn activate muscles in the arm and hand." [3]

What about walking? Don't get me started on how we walk! Your part in it is only to decide to do the action, and God handles the rest. So it's all more God's success than yours!

Inherited Cultural Instincts and Disciplines

We all inherit traits and instincts from our parents and ancestors. Some are physical, psychological, survivalist, economic or integrated with nature. They often give us advantages that we did nothing to earn. Utilizing them is more God's success than ours!

Sense of Humor

---

[3] ****June 1, 2016 Psychology Today, Spying on Your Brain to Move Your Hand. Ari Berkowitz.

A sense of humor can be defined as a person's ability to perceive humor or appreciate a joke. (See Oxforddictionaries.com.) This involves complex cognitive experiences. A sense of humor strengthens resiliency, and helps us deal more effectively with the ups and downs of life. Humor is more God's success than ours, especially at 7 am in the morning!

Intelligence

Intelligence is your logic and understanding of your environment, as well as your ability to integrate information in various contexts, including drawing from your experience. Intelligence gives you the ability to understand the apps on your smart phone. Intelligence is most commonly associated with problemsolving. Using your intelligence is more God's success than yours!

Mindfulness

Mindfulness helps us to decide what to focus on given the situation. For example, picture yourself attempting to professionally edit a video, while you look at texts from your ex, and at the same time you get a Facebook live video of a friend who has jumped off a cliff in a flight suit and is soaring over the Amazon Rain Forest at sixty miles per hour. Your mindfulness will come in to save the day and tell you that you are attempting to focus on too much, and help you to focus on what is most important.

Practicing mindfulness is more God's success than yours!

Love

To love is to care for others, and have their welfare be of paramount concern to you. It is to be fully-present for others, and committed to helping them have the best life ever. That's more God's success than yours!

Talents

Call it flair, aptitude, facility, gift, knack, technique, touch, bent, expertise, capacity – these are words we often use when we think of "talent." Here are some talents, which you might appreciate in yourself or others:

Teaching

Mechanical Aptitude

Sports

Writing

Editing

Cooking

Building

Business

Singing

Playing an instrument

Directing

Producing

Organizing

Gardening

Acting

Comedy

Caring for others

Leading

Problem-solving

Researching

What's My Part?

You might say "so with all of this God stuff, where is my part?" Good question. In everything, you have to do your part! In his brilliant book, *The War of Art*, Pressfield stresses the importance of a person's commitment to his or her art on a daily basis. Pressfield writes that the difference between a pro and an amateur is that the amateur waits for inspiration, and the pro knows that by doing the work, the inspiration will come.[4] I did the work to write this book – I sat down every day and wrote for about an hour, but I depended on inspiration, motivation, talent, and physical ability in order to do it, which was created by God. In short, whenever I use my talents and abilities, I acknowledge my part, but give God most of the credit.

Why do I do this and suggest you do this? An ordinary experience will become spiritually-rich when we acknowledge God's part, which in the moment becomes much stronger than the hyper-critical voice within us that wants us to be miserable! Spiritual energy is the only energy that is strong enough for us to stop beating ourselves up.

Chapter 7 Summary

- Some incredible things have happened that demonstrate that there is a powerful, good force in the universe that does ultimately defeat the bad in the world. When people believe in that force, and do the footwork to defeat evil, amazing things have happened.
- Use whatever words you would like to name this positive spiritual energy in you and outside of you. I use the word "God" in this book as the name for this spiritual energy, but please substitute in whatever word that resonates with you.
- You have a choice in the way you live every day: It's either

---

[4] The War of Art. Published by Black Irish Entertainment, 2012. Steven Pressfield.

living by fear or faith. Fear is what always drives beating yourself up. Faith will build you up, no matter what!

- Spiritual energy underlies our talents and abilities.
- Everything we do is more God's success than ours.
- Spiritual energy is the only energy that is strong enough for us to stop beating ourselves up.

Chapter 8

"Powerfirmations™"

A Powerfirmation™ is a word I coined which simply combines an affirmation and a prayer together. Practicing Powerfirmations™ gives us the higher-level consciousness that affirmations cannot provide because of the prayer component in Powerfirmations™. The prayer brings the spiritual energy into your consciousness which gives you increased personal power. Every time you do a Powerformation, ™ a new neural pathway is being formed which will make you stronger!

Powerfirmations™ can be used for multiple purposes, which I will describe in this chapter and the following chapters of this book. Like Autosuggestions, they need to be said out loud, with complete focus, and with emotion to be most effective.

Powerfirmations™ for Acknowledging the Small and Big Things We Do

One type of Powerfirmation™ acknowledges the positive things we do. "Good job (Insert Your Name) for successfully (Insert the positive thing you did)! I'm proud of me, and that's more God's success than mine!" This is the basic formula for saying the Powerfirmation for acknowledging the small and big positive things we do. Remember, our old brain, the Amygdala, is hyper-sensitive to emotion, so when we're saying with emotion "Good Job! I'm proud of me and that's more God's success than mine," it feels it "loud and clear!"

"Good Job!"

For many years I noticed one of the signs of good parents was how they related to their children after they did simple tasks. Good parents frequently say "Good job!!!" That's right - those two simple words! I never heard them from my parents, and I suspect you never heard or heard them enough from yours. And our parents never heard them enough from their parents!

Yes, this lack of saying "Good job" often goes back in a family's history for hundreds of years. I believe this is because parents can only give to their children what was given to them. There is also a global ignorance as to the building or destroying power of words. Many parents feel that "if it was good enough for me (and we're talking about lack of positive-acknowledgement), then it's good enough for you!"

You might be thinking: "Andrew, why do I need to say 'Good Job' for doing small things?"

Here is my response: We have beaten ourselves up over many small things, so in order to undo all of the damage we created in our consciousness, we need to build ourselves up for every small good thing that we do!

You also might be saying to yourself: "Why do I need to say 'Good job' and not say 'Good work?' 'Good job' is usually said to kids, and I am no longer a kid!"

My response is that we all have a kid inside our subconscious, and that kid needs to be reassured and commended by us adults, so that is why I suggest saying "Good job" and not "Good work."

In short, it's our responsibility to say to ourselves "Good job, (your name), for doing (insert activity), and that's more God's success than mine!" It's such a simple and beautiful acknowledgement of effort and life.

"I'm Proud of Me!"

The other words you most likely didn't hear enough when you were growing up are:

"I'm so proud of you!" For many people, they rarely heard these words, at all.

Ok, you're probably saying, "Why would I be proud of me for doing simple things such as standing in a room or opening up my eyes?" The reason is that you're practicing a healthy discipline of commending yourself and giving God most of the credit. You have to tell yourself "I'm proud of me" out loud as a replacement for the negative beating yourself up voice.

"More God's Success than Mine"

Saying "More God's success than mine" is the *Power* in the Powerfirmation™. I'm acknowledging my part, but giving God most of the credit. Why do I do this and suggest you do this? As I discussed in Chapter 8, an ordinary experience will become a spiritually-rich experience when we acknowledge God's part, which in the moment becomes much stronger than the hypercritical voice within us that wants us to be miserable!

The Art of Powerfirmations™

Ok, put down this book right now! I mean you! Yeah you, the person reading this! Just stop and go into a room where you're alone.

Good. *Now, just say out loud:*

"Good job (Insert Your Name) for successfully (Insert the small thing that you did – For example, successfully standing in the room). I'm proud of me, and that's more God's success than mine!" Now, do it again!

Congratulations, you just did a healthy exercise that will build you up unconditionally! You may be more relaxed at this moment, and you may feel positive spiritual/emotional energy in your body. Some of my clients tell me that they find this exercise to be somewhat humorous, which lightens up their mood.

Now find five mundane tasks that you do every day and say outloud Powerfirmations for each task.

Ok, so here is an example. Let's say your name is Fred. You would be saying "Good job (Fred) for successfully getting out of bed! I'm proud of me, and that's more God's success than mine!" Here are more examples:

"Good job (Trish), for successfully separating the cat from the goldfish! I'm proud of me, and *** that's more God's success than mine!"

"Good job (Phil), for successfully paying the bill! I'm proud of me, and that's more God's success than mine!"

"Good job (Matt) for successfully petting the cat! I'm proud of me, and that's more God's success than mine!"

"Good job (Terri) for successfully boarding the ferry! I'm proud of me, and that's more God's success than mine!"

You get the idea! Please note that you don't need to make your Powerfirmations™ rhyme. I included rhyme in these examples just for fun.

Healthy Disciplines/Toxic Indulgences

Beating yourself up is a toxic indulgence! Building yourself up is a healthy discipline! Never thought about it that way, did you?

Well, you will now!

So what does discipline mean?

Unfortunately, you most likely equate discipline with punishment that you received in school from your parents and what you learned in boot camp or working in a telemarketing call center for hearing aids. Or you might equate discipline with staying away from eating strawberry cheesecake or being on Facebook three hours a day!

In this book I am using a different meaning for the word "discipline." I use one of the definitions listed in Vocabulary.com: "a system of rules of conduct or method of practice."

The term "Healthy Discipline" as used in this book is just good stuff you do regularly. You could actually say that petting your cat is a discipline!

Here are some examples of Healthy Disciplines:

a) Walking your dog before he has an accident on your favorite sofa!

b) Studying for a test when you actually planned to study!

c) Spending time with loved ones and not checking your email every two minutes!

Now, write down your Healthy Disciplines.

Here are some examples of Toxic Indulgences:

a) Binging on so much junk food that your waist size is increasing faster than your blood pressure!

b) Watching so much TV that you don't know where the story ends and you begin!

c) Having a pity party that is so intense that you wear out two teddy bears!

Now, write down your Toxic Indulgences.

_____

_____

_____

_____

_____

_____

The Art of Powerfirmations™ Is a Healthy Discipline

The practice of Powerfirmations™ is a Healthy Discipline that is easy to practice – Powerfirmations™ need to be said at least four times per day. Why do they need to be said four times per day? You need to do this because your "Museum States ™" are very old! If you're forty, they are at least thirty-five years old. If you're twenty, they are at least fifteen years old. Your day is very long. For most of us, it's at least sixteen hours. Your day is like a play in four acts. What I mean by the word "day" is the time you're not sleeping. Oftentimes our morning is totally different from the afternoon – there is a different energy and form, and the evening is totally distinct from the afternoon and the night. So Powerfirmations™ have to be said *with emotion at least four times a day* to create healthy new habits which will generate better choices.

It has been said that when we wake up, we are engaged in the most difficult transition of the day – we are moving from our dream world to the reality of our lives. If we have a problem with anger, anxiety or fear, we wake up with beating ourselves up. This has been true for me and is true for millions of people. It is essential for me, and many of my clients and workshop participants, to say a "Powerfirmation™" when we first wake up in the morning. It's of paramount importance that you do the same. Saying a Powerfirmation first thing in the morning will interrupt beating ourselves up thoughts and create a better reality for the day!

Even though it's hard to talk in the first fifteen seconds of the day, do a mumbling and bumbling Powerformation ™. For example, if your second thought is "I need to do laundry today," say out loud: "Good job thinking the thought 'need to do the laundry!' I'm proud of me, (   ), and that's more God's success than mine!" If your second thought is "got to feed the cat," you would day out loud; "Good job thinking the thought 'need to feed the cat!" I'm proud of me, (   ), and that's more God's success than mine!"

This is a million times better than listening to the toxic critical voices in your head that you've heard hundreds of times.

Even if you don't experience any beating yourself up when you wake up in the morning, and your mind feels like an empty space, it's still important to say a Powerfirmation within the first thirty seconds of awakening. "Nature abhors a vacuum," so it's important to program your brain with a positive dose of spiritual energy by saying a Powerfirmation.

The more you do these exercises, the easier it will be to build yourself up and resist the temptation of putting yourself down. Then you will be more relaxed and centered with your friends, family, clients, customers, and audience! It's like practicing an instrument or martial arts, the more you do it, the better you'll get!

For you to get the maximum results from this book, you have to do your part, and share the Powerfirmations™ with others as much as possible. Then, the power you get from these exercises will be the strongest in you. So, if this is going to work for you, you have to do your part!

Does that seem like a lot? Listen, saying four Powerfirmations™ each day takes a total of one to two minutes. I have seen Powerfirmations™ work extremely effectively for my clients and workshop participants to create a higher quality of consciousness, which helps them to make better choices. Isn't it worth a couple of minutes to build yourself up, and make better choices than you ever did before? The quick answer is yes!

One of the benefits of you building yourself up on a daily basis is earning the state of positive expectancy – you will more often be looking forward to each day. Just like doing martial arts or going to the gym, if you regularly and often do Powerfirmations™, you'll be growing "new building yourself up muscles."

Self-Care Is God's Care

In order to have a higher consciousness, it's important to always remember that self-care is God's care. Saying Powerfirmations ™ is a great way to take care of ourselves emotionally and spiritually. It is also essential that we remember to take care of our physical state. If you find that you are hungry, tired, or fatigued, ***then eat, rest, sleep or go for a walk. Do your laundry. Clean your home. Enjoy positive entertainment, such as listening to music or watching a good movie. Or take the day off. This will always bring you back to a stronger place.

In the following chapters I will describe how to use Powerfirmations™ to successfully get out of Museum States™, cope with life's problems and mistakes you have made, and set and reach goals.

Chapter 8 Summary

- The level of consciousness you currently have is more important than your age or education, the amount of money you have or don't have, or which side of the tracks you were born on.
- A Powerfirmation™ combines an affirmation and a prayer together.
- Practicing Powerfirmations™ gives us the higher-level consciousness that affirmations cannot provide because of the prayer component in Powerfirmations™. The prayer brings the spiritual energy into your consciousness which gives you increased personal power.
- Like Autosuggestions, Powerfirmations™ need to be said out loud, with complete focus, and with emotion to be most effective.
- Powerfirmations™ can be used for multiple purposes.
- One type of Powerfirmation™ acknowledges the positive big and small things we do.
- It's important for us to often say to ourselves "Good job" and "I'm proud of me," because we did not feedback from our parents when we were growing up.
- Saying "More God's success than mine" is the *Power* in the Powerfirmation™.
- The practice of Powerfirmations™ is an art that is easy to practice – they need to be said at least four times per day, especially when you get up in the morning.

Chapter 9

Hey, You Can Leave Your Position as the Curator of Your Museum States™!

How to "Spot and Catch" a Museum State™

One of the ways you'll know you're going into a Mu-seum State" ™ during the day is a feeling of a creepy fear or obsession, or panic, or a feeling of gloom that suddenly comes over or out of you, seemingly out of nowhere. You, may have a feeling in your body that the sky is about to fall. For me, I sometimes feel this cringe and fear in my gut while I'm sitting there trying to enjoy a beautiful day, and I spot right away that I am in the "Gloom and Doomer™" state. Other times you may know the source that triggered the Museum State™.

Museum States™ start with a feeling; then they may go into a sequence of negative thoughts; and then possibly into a behavior. You need to leave your volunteer position as the Curator of your Museum States™ and, instead, be committed to "spotting and catching" them from the moment they spring up! In so doing, you're living in a relational way instead of a reactive way. An example of a reactive choice is to feel one of these negative feelings and head for the vending machine, and mega-dose on candy bars. This may give you temporary relief, but not for long. Pretty soon one of your Museum States™ will return, and all that will happen is that you'll feel that your pants are shrinking!

So your best navigational course is to acknowledge that this feeling is occurring, and then "catch it" by doing a Powerfirmation™ specific for this Museum State ™, which for the Gloom and Doomer™ is: "Thank you, God, for letting me know the sky is where it's supposed to be, and that you have me in the palm of your hand for at least the next four hours. You didn't take me this far to drop me! Good job (   ). I'm proud of me, and that's more God's success than mine!

Imagine you're sitting in your office - it's a beautiful day, and you see an unlimited blue sky with white clouds gliding gracefully, and seals scampering playfully in the harbor. There is a feeling of peace and joy that clearly others are experiencing. You suddenly have this feeling that "the other shoe is going to drop," with anxiety running up and down your spine or a tension in your stomach. You could be "opening the door" to the Museum State™ of the "Panicker™", which at this exact moment, you are seeking out. So, your job is to acknowledge that this feeling is occurring, and then "catch it" by doing a Powerfirmation™ specific for this Museum State ™. "Thank you, God, for allowing me to be comfortable with relaxation and ease at least for the next four hours. Good job (   )! I'm proud of me and that's more God's success than mine! Or, good Job Andrew for seeing my fear objectively and successfully but God, that's more our success than mine!"

Powerfirmations™ for catching and stopping Museum States™ can and will improve your mood very quickly.

Powerfirmations ™ for Catching and Stopping Every Museum State™

Below are Powerfirmations™ for every "Museum State ™ listed

in Chapter 7. These will help you quickly get out of your Museum States™. I recommend that you say Powerfirmations™ for each of the Museum States™ that applies to you four times each day.

The words used in these Powerfirmations™ are suggested only. If you find that there are other words you would like to add or substitute that resonate with you, by all means, do so!

Doing Powerfirmations™ regularly and frequently creates positive feelings and new spiritual thought patterns which, in turn, generate healthier neural pathways that will help you to make better choices. Remember to say them <u>out loud</u>! You can say them with your eyes open or closed, whatever works best for you.

For Being a LessThaner™

Thank you, God, for allowing me to feel more than enough for at least the next four hours. Good job ( )! I'm proud of me, and that's more God's success than mine!

For Being a Struggleaholic™ or an Angst-glutton™

Thank you, God, for giving me ease, peace, fun and success for at least the next four hours. Good job ( )! I'm proud of me, and that's more God's success than mine!

For Being a Crumbaholic™ or a Misery-Maven™

Thank you, God, for allowing me to experience prosperity, love and joy for the next four hours. Good job ( )! I'm proud of me, and that's more God's success than mine!

For the Worrier

Thank you, God, for helping me to see possible solutions and to focus on good outcomes for at least the next four hours. Good job ( )! I'm proud of me, and that's more God's success than mine!

For the Gloom and Doomer™

Thank you, God, for letting me know that the sky is where it's supposed to be, and that you have me in the palm of your hand. You didn't take me this far to drop me! Good job (   )! I'm proud of me, and that's more God's success than mine!

For the Panicker ™

Thank you, God, for allowing me to be relaxed and ease at least for the next four hours. Good job (   )! I'm proud of me and that's more God's success than mine!

For the Crises King or Queen

Thank you, God, for helping me to navigate this difficult situation under your care and love. Good job (   )! I'm proud of me, and that's more God's success than mine!

For the Superhuman

Thank you, God, for allowing me to know at least for the next four hours that only by taking care of myself first, can I be of service to you and to others. Good job (   )! I'm proud of me, and that's more God's success than mine!

For the Eggshell Walker ™

Thank you, God, for allowing me for at least the next four hours to not seek out abusive people and to allow into my life positive people. Good job (   )! I'm proud of me, and that's more God's success than mine!

For Mr. and Ms. Guilty

Thank you, God, for letting me know that I am not responsible for all of the troubles around me, that there is more good in me than bad, and for giving me courage and wisdom to stand up for myself for at least the next four hours. Good job (   )! I'm proud of me, and that's more God's success than mine!

For the Edge-Meister ™

Thank you, God, for helping me to be considerate to myself and others in the use of my money and time for at least the next four hours. Good job (   )! I'm proud of me and that's more God's success than mine!

For The Perfectionist

Thank you, God, for helping me to be aware of my perfectionism and to see that I'll be happier and have better relationships if I let it go for at least the next four hours. Good job ( )! I'm proud of me and that's more God's success than mine!

For The Snobaholic ™

Thank you, God, for allowing me to be a friend among friends and a worker among workers at least for the next four hours. Good job (   )! I'm proud of me, and that's more God's success than mine!

For The Control Freak

Thank you, God, for helping me to be aware of my compulsion to be in control and to see that I'll be safer and have better relationships if I let it go. Good job (   )! I'm proud of me and that's more God's success than mine!

For The Rageaholic

Thank you, God, for helping me to remember, at least for the next four hours, to have a sense of humor and to let go of my anger, so that I'll be safer and happier. Good job (   )! I'm proud of me and that's more God's success than mine!

For The Pleaser

Thank you, God, for letting me know at least for the next four hours that my work and my actions are ultimately for you, and it's most important that I respect myself always.

Good job (   )! I'm proud of me and that's more God's success than mine!

For the Nitpicker™

Thank you, God, for helping me to focus on the good around me and to understand that the greater my acceptance, the greater my peace of mind! Good job (   )! I'm proud of me and that's more God's success than mine!

Throughout the day, one "Museum State™" can flow into another in you, like cloud formations across the sky. Powerfirmations™ ensure that "the sun" shines in your life even though some clouds did appear.

What Kind of Story Are You Telling Yourself?

You can tell yourself a fear or faith story. In either case the one that you commit to daily, sooner or later will come true. It's either one or the other. The negative fear-based story will create a bad process. The positive faith-based story will create a good process. A good process is necessary to create success; a bad process will generally create failure.

All stories are accepted as fact by your old brain (the amygdala) and your subconscious, which is why we emotionally react when we see a comedy, or drama. Our old brain cannot make the distinction between a story and reality.

You may be thinking "Andrew, I feel dishonest saying that I have accomplished something when I haven't yet done so. Many of your Powerfirmations™ seem to suggest that I do this." Some of my workshop participants have expressed the same sentiment to me. Well, here is my answer: What we anticipate, we get! If I wake up saying "I know I'm going to have a crappy day," then I will have a crappy day. If I wake up saying "Thank you, God, for giving me ease, peace, fun and success for at least the next four hours. Good job, Andrew! I'm proud of me, and that's more God's success than mine!" Then the chances are increased that I will have a good day, because what we anticipate we get!

Statements that Can Trigger You to Go into Your Museum States™

Word choices and word groupings can trigger you to seek out one or more of your Museum States™. For example, take the common phrases "You screwed up!" "You only have yourself to blame!" "I totally blame you!" "It's all your fault!!" These statements can propel you into the Museum State™ of being a LessThaner™, Crumbaholic™, or Mr. or Ms. Guilty. "If you love me, you'll do this for me!" This sentence is perfect for bringing you right into the Museum States of the Superhuman and Pleaser. "If you don't get your act together, you are out of here!

This statement can trigger you to go into the Museum State of being a Struggleaholic™ or Panicker.

The tone and word groups that people carelessly use can make difficult situations much worse. So, how do you protect yourself when someone in a business or personal relationship uses word groups that trigger you? My answer is to immediately use Powerfirmations™ for the Museum States that are being activated in you!

Creating a Combination Powerfirmation™

You might be thinking, "This is impossible, I have *so many* Museum States™ - I won't be able to say all the applicable Powerfirmations™ four times a day!"

Well, there is a solution! You can create a Combination Powerfirmation™. For example, for the LessThaner™, Worrier™, and Stuggleaholic™, you might say: "Thank you, God, for helping me to feel more than enough and to see possible solutions and focus on good outcomes, and giving me ease, peace, fun and success for at least the next four hours. Good job (.............)! I'm proud of me, and that's more God's success than mine!"

Build Yourself Up Without Limits

Here is a story that illustrates the power of using a Combination Powerfirmation.™

Let ME Eat Crumbs?

You're a marketing executive for your firm, and a client calls you to make a presentation to his boss for a wider product distribution within his company. You fly into the city where the national headquarters is located. The CEO and Chief Financial Officer are waiting for you. You get your rental car, and while you're driving there, your thoughts are going like this:

"Wow, this is potentially the biggest account I've ever had. If I blow it, my job could be on the line! I'm so anxious, I can taste it. I need to relax, but I can't. Yeah, but they're going to want a great deal and there is so much competition out there - why do they want to do business with me anyway? I bet you it's because I give their district office a 20% discount, and my boss says I don't have to, but I do. Wow, they are going to want even more! I know it, but how much do I have left to give? Just another 6 percent! With my luck they're going to want a 25% discount - that leaves me with only a 1% commission!!!"

You walk into the meeting, and your company and product are attacked six ways to Wednesday, and you become defensive instead of building value. By the time you get to price, they ask for a whopping 26% discount. At this point, you feel a shaky and ask: "Where is the Men's Room?"

When you enter the Men's Room, you see that you are alone and you suddenly realize that your Museum States™ have been activated: The LessThaner™, The Struggleaholic™, and The Crumbaholic™. You immediately say a Combination Powerfirmation: "Thank you, God, for allowing me to feel more than enough; helping me to have ease, peace and success; and giving me prosperity, love and fun, for at least the next four hours. Good job, David! I'm proud of me, and that's more God's success than mine!" Immediately, you think fun? You gotta be kidding - I'm getting beaten up on price! Then you remembered that football game you watched yesterday and how much you enjoyed seeing your football team come from behind and win the game. You then and there decide to go back into that meeting and fight back!

You go back into the meeting, and you tell the CEO and CFO five value-building points for your company and product, and you can see that they are impressed. You further let them know what they will be losing if they go to your competitors. You tell them that 20% is the maximum discount that you can give, and you rarely give this large of a discount, but you are willing to do it for them because of the volume potential. You immediately propose a high volume sale with a 20% discount. They try to negotiate with you and ask for a 23% discount. You again repeat that a 20% discount is the lowest you can go. The CEO and CFO then look at each other stunned!

Then, the CEO smiles and says OK, you got yourself a deal! He signs your contract, and says "Dave, you really impressed me with your turn-around in your presentation. What did you take back there – you came out of there like a new man! Tell me your secret." You turn and tell them: "Well, actually I didn't take anything. What I did was totally legal. I had a good conversation with the Big Guy Upstairs!" They smile, and the CEO says "Understood. Thank you for sharing that with us. Pleasure dealing with you. Look forward to talking to you soon." Then you shake hands with the CEO and CFO, and you leave the office.

You get into your rental car, call your significant other, and tell her: "Hi Julie, You won't believe it! I closed an amazing deal with the largest account I have ever had, and it truly was more God's success than mine! I'm racing to make my plane flight, so I'll tell you more when I see you at the airport. Love you. Bye."

OK. It's your turn now. Please go ahead and write out some

Combination Powerfirmations™ that will work for you, so you can refer back to them easily until you memorize them.

_____

_____

_____

_____

_____

_____

Mini-Powerfirmations™

Sometimes within the day, given the amount of stress, conflict, confrontation, or just automobile traffic that's backed up, you might not have the "bandwidth" to do complete Powerfirmations™. You may be going into a tense meeting, confrontation, or interview or be in another difficult situation and feel that you are going into a Museum State (always triggered by fear). There may also be times where you are so tangled up in your feelings that you are having a tough time trying to determine what Museum State™ is being triggered in you. Not to worry, and of course, worry is a Museum State! Mini-Powerfirmations™ will work in a stressful moment to bring you right back to the positive state of faith and peace. As always, they need to be said out loud with as much emotion as possible. Your amygdala is always willing to go along with what you say out loud with emotion. Repeat each Mini-Powerfirmation™ one to five times.

Here are some examples of Mini-Powerfirmations™:

*** Thank you, God, for helping me to get calm!

Thank you, God, for helping me to relax!

Thank you, God, for handling this problem!

Thank you, God, for giving me guidance on how to handle this problem!

Thank you, God, for helping me to stay in life and exit my Museum States™!

Thank you, God, for letting me know that I am more than enough!

Thank you, God, for letting me know that it's safe to leave home!

Thank you, God, for letting me know that I'm not alone!

Thank you, God, for giving me ease, peace, fun and success!

Thank you, God, for letting me know that it's safe to move on!

Thank you, God, for letting me know that it's safe to be me!

Thank you, God, for letting me know that it's safe to feel!

Thank you, God, for letting me know that I need to take care of me!

Thank you, God, for letting me know that it's safe to be present!

Thank you, God, for letting me know that it's safe to love!

Thank you, God, for letting me know that it's safe to be loved!

Thank you, God, for letting me know that I can be loved just as I am!

Thank you, God, for letting me know that it's OK to make mistakes and learn from them!

Thank you, God, for letting me know that it's safe for me to move ahead!

Thank you, God, for letting me know that I deserve to be prosperous!

Mini-Powerfirmations™ will always improve your current state, since you are "turbo injecting faith!"

Transit Vehicles

There are five transit vehicles that are like shuttles or buses that bring us back to Museum State Avenue in two to three seconds. These transit vehicles take us out of being present in our reality. They tend to come up for us, especially when we are hungry, angry or anxious, lonely or tired (HALT). Powerfirmations can be effectively used to help us to not get on the bus or shuttle destined to Museum State Avenue. A Powerfirmation is a transit vehicle that will instead bring us to Prosperity Boulevard, allowing us to be fully present.

Beating Yourself Up

"I'm such a loser – there's nothing good about me. No matter what I do, it does not work out. This is an example of beating yourself up, which will take you instantaneously to your top Museum States. In order to not use this transit vehicle destined toward your Museum States, immediately say a Powerfirmation such as this: "Thank you, God, for letting me know that you have given me assets, and I'm worthy of success. I will succeed with your help and help from others. Good job (   )! I'm proud of me, and that's more God's success than mine!"

Sand-trap Thinking

"I can't believe I made that mistake! I can't believe I did it again!" This is an example of sand-trap thinking. Sand-trap thinking is when your mind goes over and over a mistake you made or a project that crashed and you don't see a solution or resolution. It is caused by fear. To counter this thinking, say a Powerfirmation such as this: "Thank you, God, for helping me to have patience when I have repeated a mistake and the wisdom to lay out a plan so I don't make the mistake again."

Negative Endowment

"I failed the test to be a (   ), and that means that I'm not cut out for it." This is an example of negative endowment, which is putting negative emotional energy and belief into an experience or series of experiences that do not warrant it. Clearly the person in this situation could have looked at the same experience in a positive light, decided to get a tutor and then to re-take the exam. When this thinking begins to crop up, it's important to say a Powerfirmation such as this: "Thank you, God, for letting me know that I don't need to be perfect and if I continue to work hard and get support from others, I will achieve my goals."

Compare and Despair

"She's making three times the money I am making and works less hours!"

Compare and despair is when we see another person doing better than us, and we compare ourselves to them and feel incompetent or less than enough. We can do this with our friends, family, co-workers or even celebrities! It's a set-up for us to guess what? You got it! Beat ourselves up! It is a transit device that quickly returns us to our top Museum States, especially the Misery Maven, Gloom and Doomer and the Angst Glutton.

We can easily get triggered into "Compare and Despair" when we read about the amazing successes of celebrities.

Do you think that celebrities "have it made?" Well, many don't. They may look good from the outside, but reading about the latest celebrity divorce, melt-down, bankruptcy or drug overdose gives us the awareness that all is not always "golden" behind those mansion doors.

Celebrities are people just like us who have real challenges, fears, pain, resentments, and conflict that can cause them sometimes to make self-destructive choices.

When we hear of their demise or latest trouble, we're shocked that people with their wealth, talent, and fame could do such a thing. But, they are people like us who get up every morning and have to face their day, just as we do. They, like us, have to face the question "Am I going to beat myself down or build myself up without limits?"

In addition to being triggered by reading about celebrities, we can also be triggered when we hear of our friend or family member's success such as getting a great promotion, buying a new car or house, or getting married. This will most likely bring up a feeling of being "less-than" in yourself.

So how do we prevent ourselves from getting into the "Compare and Despair Shuttle toward Museum State Avenue?"

Here is the answer:

1. Do not compare yourself to anyone except for yourself!
2. Say a Powerfirmation such as, "Thank you, God, for giving me gratitude for what I do and guidance and willingness to take the right actions to reach my goals. Good job (   )! I'm proud of me, and that's more God's success than mine!"

Screenwriting

"Screenwriting" creates a step by step scenario in the future that always creates a negative result for us. One of the ways we return to our Museum States™ is through the transit vehicle of negative screenwriting. We become screenwriters in our heads in life situations in which we find ourselves. This unsane screenwriting starts involuntarily, although with the right tools it can be immediately stopped. This reminds me of an old joke I heard many years ago.

The Jack Screenplay

Build Yourself Up Without Limits

One day, a salesman is driving along and he gets a flat tire. He opens the trunk of his car and, much to his dismay he discovers he does not have a jack. He starts walking, and one mile down the road he sees a farmhouse. While walking to it, he begins to think "Wow, this farmer might have a gun. He could actually rob me! Or, he might be calling the sheriff right now. It could be all over the news! Or, what if he's part of some cult of wacko farmers? With my luck, I'll miss my big sales presentation in two hours and I'll get fired. Then, my wife will divorce me and my kid will go on drugs!" The salesman finally gets to the farmhouse, knocks on the door, and an old farmer answers: "Hello, young man, can I help you?" The salesman looks at him and shouts "keep your (bleeping) Jack!"

It's an old joke, but how different is it really from the thinking most of us do without thinking! We don't see that we're choosing to stress ourselves out and put ourselves down. This then creates a negative self-fulfilling prophecy. Even though the person who wrote the joke was not thinking of Museum States™, the guy in the joke could have been seeking out the Rageaholic, Struggleaholic™, Crises King and/or Misery-Maven™ Museum States ™ because he was afraid of being in the life situation he was presented.

So what drives the writing of the negative screenplay in your head? The answer is fear - fear of losing what you have or not getting what you want. In the Jack Joke example, the salesman was afraid of not getting to his appointment on time, losing his job, and losing his family, so he created one negative scene in his head after another. That type of fear is like a big thunderstorm with lightning which becomes so scary that we run into our "old dilapidated Museum State™ house." This is the same way we would run into our actual home if we as children were in a thunderstorm, even if that home just contained a drunk father, a depressed, chain-smoking mother, and a hungry goldfish.

So here is the basic pattern of what is occurring in you:

BIG FEAR AND/OR ANGER causes you to WRITE NEGATIVE SCREENPLAY IN YOUR HEAD, which returns you to YOUR MUSEUM STATE™ (Struggleaholic, Rageaholic, LessThaner, Perfectionist, etc.). This leads you to DESTRUCTIVE CHOICES AND ACTIONS OR INACTIONS ….

You may say: "It seems dumb to do this unhealthy screenwriting," and you're right! However, intelligence is only as good as the spiritual condition that surrounds it.

How do you stop this unsane screenwriting? Simple, you build up your spiritual condition with a Powerfirmation™. The second you catch yourself negatively screenwriting, stop it immediately with a Powerfirmation™ such as this: "Thank you, God, for giving me the strength to stop my unsane screenwriting. Good job ( )! I'm proud of me, and that's more God's success than mine!" Or you can simply say this out loud: "Stop screenwriting! Good job ( )! I'm proud of me, and that's more God's success than mine!" Then follow it right away with a Powerfirmation™ for one of your Museum States™ or a Combination Powerfirmation™ for multiple Museum States™.

In the story above about David, the marketing executive who ultimately decided to not choose crumbs, if he had spotted his unsane screenwriting immediately while he was driving, then used Powerfirmations™ to stop the toxic screenwriting, he would have had a much better start to his business meeting.

OK. Write out a recent unsane screenplay in your head and the Powerfirmation(s)™ you plan to use the next time you start negatively screenwriting.

_____

_____

_____

_____

_____

_____

_____

_____

_____

_____

_____

_____

_____

The Power of Objectivity

When an airliner flies too close to the mountains, a warning buzzer goes off in the cockpit to alert the pilots to take corrective action so they don't crash into the mountains. A therapist once said to me: "You can't stop doing something until you see yourself doing it." By practicing Powerfirmations™ at least four times a day, and sharing them with others, we increase our power of objectivity so that when we are about to enter a Museum State™, a warning buzzer goes off in our brains which tells us that we are flying "too close to the mountains," and we need to take corrective action. The more you do Powerfirmations™, the greater your awareness and power to avoid entering your Museum States™! My clients and workshop participants, who say Powerfirmations regularly at least four times a day, report that over time they have experienced an 80 – 95% reduction in their entry into their Museum States. The same will hold true for you!

A way to help you to see clearly and objectively how Museum States™ keep you in bondage, and the effectiveness of

Powerfirmations™ in helping you to get out of that bondage, is to visualize Museum States™ as handcuffs and Powerfirmations™ as the keys to unlocking the handcuffs.

Chapter 9 Summary

- We can leave our "curator of Museum States" position with Powerfirmations designed for each Museum State.
- Museum States™ start with a feeling. Your best navigational course is to acknowledge that this feeling is occurring, and then "catch it" by doing a Powerfirmation™ for the specific Museum State ™.
- Saying Powerfirmations™ for your Museum States™ will immediately improve your mood and choices.
- There are Powerfirmations™ for quickly catching and stopping every "Museum State ™.
- Saying Powerfirmations™ regularly and frequently (e.g. four times per day) for Museum States™ that apply to you creates positive feelings and new spiritual thought patterns which, in turn, generate healthier neural pathways that will help you to make better choices.
- The negative fear-based story will create a bad result. The positive faith-based story will create a good result.
- If you have a lot of Museum States™, you can create a Combination Powerfirmation. ™
- At a given time, if you feel that you are going into a Museum State™ and don't have the "bandwidth" to do a complete Powerfirmation™, then say a Mini-Powerfirmation.™ It will work in a stressful moment to bring you right back to the positive state of faith and peace.
- There are five transit vehicles that quickly bring us back to our top Museum States in two to three seconds: (1) Beating yourself up, (2) Sand-trap thinking, (3) Negative Endowment, (4) Compare and Despair, and (5) Screenwriting. These transit vehicles take us out of being

present in our reality.

- Powerfirmations can be effectively used to help us to not get on the bus or shuttle destined to Museum State Avenue. A Powerfirmation is a transit vehicle that will instead bring us to Prosperity Boulevard, allowing us to be fully present.
- The more you do Powerfirmations™, the greater your awareness and power to avoid entering your Museum States™!

Chapter 10

A Conversation Without Condemnation!

What We Speak, We Create elf-love is not restricted to actions such as doing yoga, watching the sun come up or sticking to a food plan. A deep expression of self-love is communicating relation-

Sally to ourselves by talking out loud to ourselves in a supportive way without beating ourselves up. When fear, anger and resentments are hurting us, it is easy to become reactive. Meaning, there is a good chance that we will take self-destructive actions if we don't talk about the situation with ourselves and build ourselves up unconditionally in the process. When we are reactive, we make snap decisions out of fear or survival. When we are relational, we take time to relate to ourselves regarding a decision, and the more relational we are, the better the decision. My suggestion is that you install in your walking-around consciousness a "relational app," meaning, you talk things through <u>out</u> <u>loud</u> with kindness toward yourself as a new habit, knowing your daily focus is to go from fear to faith. The more you go from fear to faith, the more your life will improve.

Here are examples of the difference between "relational" and "reactive" responses to the same situation:

Situation 1: You suspect that your boyfriend or girlfriend might be having an affair.

Reactive Response: You punch your fist through a wall and break a few knuckles.

Relational Response: You say out loud to yourself "Look I know I'm upset. What is the most generous and considerate thing I can do for myself right now?"

Situation 2: You get a big tax bill in the mail.

Reactive Response: You start eating a couple of scoops of ice cream because you feel that you're entitled to have a little comfort food, and you wind up eating the whole gallon. Now you feel like a big pig!

Relational Response: You say out loud. "Ok, I know this is upsetting. I will put the tax bill on my desk, and talk to my accountant about this tomorrow. I need to chill right now."

Situation 3: Your ex bought airplane tickets to take the kids away for a holiday ski weekend, when you expected to take them camping. You have put in three hours of time planning the trip.

Reactive Response: You go to a bar with the intention of only having two drinks to "take the edge off," you keep drinking and get totally plastered, and you feel like crap the next day.

Relational Response: You say out loud, "Good job wanting to give my children this great experience. I'm sorry I didn't let my ex know sooner that my plans were for this weekend. This is so disappointing! What is the most generous and considerate thing I can do for myself right now?"

Clearly being relational beats being reactive, and the reason for that is that being relational comes out of faith, honesty, love and consideration to us and to our family, friends and our workplace.

The important idea about relational communication is that it creates an immediate improved future. In short, it creates self-affirming actions instead of self-abusive actions.

Here is another example:

Imagine having a knock-down, drag-out fight with your wife, or ex, or whomever. You, instead of hitting the bar, refrigerator, joint, porn, or meth, say out loud: "What is the most considerate and generous thing I can do for myself right now?"

I know you're possibly thinking that what I'm suggesting sounds unrealistic, but let's break down the sequence of the process.

Reactive Response:

- Fear/anger-
- Self-destructive action-----
- Negative blowback to you.

Relational Response:

- Fear/anger
- Self-affirming communication -------------
- Increased power for you.

It's bad enough when you're having a situation in your life where anger caused by fear is triggered in you, but it only makes your situation worse, which will be filled with regret later on, to go into a self-destructive choice brought on by the fear/anger tango. On the other hand, even though it will feel awkward at first, self-affirming communication will not only stop you from harming yourself after the melt down, but will also help resolve the problem that caused the anger and fear. Self-affirming thoughts, speech and behavior broadcast your intention to God of commitment to the positive, and God takes notice! As you read on in this chapter, you will see a more complete way to employ self-care and self-affirmation after the triggering emotions of fear and anger.

Conversations with Condemnation and without Condemnation

There's nothing like something going wrong - a disappointment or an expectation that you had that didn't come to fruition - for you to "get out the club" and start whacking away on yourself with all get-out. This is not being firm with yourself; it's selfcondemnation! Staying in your head, these internal self-confrontational thoughts can get out of hand. The reason is that in emotionally-heated moments born out of fear, objectivity and balance "go out the window."

There's an old saying: "If it's hysterical, it's historical." What that means is that if you're having a melt-down over a situation, it's often triggered by an experience of abuse or neglect that you have in your memory bank. Your "old brain" has no sense of time division. In other words, if somebody yells at you now, and you have an over-reaction, that old brain of yours is still back thirty years ago where you were yelled at or ignored and, as far as it's concerned, today is the next day after thirty years ago. This type of reaction is also known as "being triggered."

Again, there is a big difference between being firm with yourself and condemning yourself. Let's explore the difference. Let's say you're a student and you're not studying enough, and your grades are suffering. This is a typical beating yourself up conversational snippet:

"If you don't get off your ass, you loser, you gonna screw it up again like you have so many times before, so get your sorry ass up to that dorm room and crack the book!!!"

"Screw it. The only thing I'm cracking open is a six pack and a bag of chips, and I'm gonna binge-watch TV!"

Now let's look at the same situation by having this Conversation without Condemnation of yourself out loud.

"So, your grades aren't good in this subject. How do you feel about that?

"I'm not feeling great, and I know I need this subject to get my degree, but most of the time I hate it! I'm also angry at myself for not doing better."

"Hey, good job being honest with me, Craig!!

"I forgive me for what I did and did not do."

"Good job forgiving yourself, Craig! So what is the most generous and considerate thing that I can do for myself right now?" "I'll study a half hour more for at least five nights a week."

"I respect that. Good job, Craig! I'm proud of me, and that's more God's success than mine!"

The difference between the conversations is that The Conversation without Condemnation is relational and involves constructive decision-making, and the other conversation is reactive, condemning and involves destructive decision-making.

When we make a reactive decision, we're "shooting from the hip." Meaning, there is no thought, just a quick reaction, which goes from not the best, to destructive. When we make a relational decision, it is the product of an honest and kind dialogue with ourselves. If your grades are suffering, beating yourself up will not help; having a Conversation without Condemnation will!

Components of the Conversation without Condemnation

To summarize, the Conversation without Condemnation is a conversation that you have with yourself after you experience an emotional upset, where you communicate relationally with honesty, kindness and constructive decision-making.

I recommend that you have the Conversation without Condemnation once or twice a day. It's important to do it as soon as possible after you feel anger, resentment or fear toward yourself or others. Practicing a Conversation without Condemnation is a discipline and, if it's going to work when you have major fear spikes in your life, it has to be "on-line" in your head. So, practice it every day regarding small difficulties, as well as the big ones!

These are the basic components of the Conversation without Condemnation:

- The whole conversation is done out loud and with you addressing yourself using your first name. Start by being in a quiet place where you feel comfortable and will be totally undisturbed.
- Begin by building yourself up by saying Powerfirmations for the small accomplishments that you do. This will generate new positive spiritual energy which creates power in the process. Ok, you get the idea and by now, you're in the "zone." You've leveraged the spiritual power of these Powerfirmations.
- State the facts of the situation in an objective way. You may want to ask yourself this question: "How much is my problem really worth - ten dollars or a thousand dollars?" Don't give a ten-dollar problem a thousand dollars' worth of energy!
- Ask yourself how you feel about the situation. Then honestly say how you feel and say "Good job ( ), for being honest! This builds spiritual energy.
- If you feel that a Museum State is being activated in you, then it's important that you say in your Conversation without Condemnation a Powerfirmation to get you out of the Museum State.

Build Yourself Up Without Limits

- For you to stay in life, it is essential that you forgive yourself for any mistakes you have made. Remember that it's OK for you to honestly see your part in causing the situation, but it's never OK for you to beat yourself up! So, you would say something like this: "I forgive me for making a mistake! Good job (   ) for successfully forgiving myself!
- Then ask yourself: "What is the most generous and considerate thing I can do for myself right now? Good job, (   )! I'm proud of me, and that's more God's success than mine!"

By saying in this conversation out loud, "Good job, (   ) I'm proud of me, and that's more God's success than mine, it's spiritually refueling the conversation. When we ask ourselves: "What is the most generous and considerate thing we can do for ourselves now?" We're in a conversation of harmony, and our old brain is totally OK with that!

Here is another example of the way you may have dealt with a disappointment before Conversations without Condemnation:

"I can't believe they cut me out of the real estate deal that I busted my butt for! I'm such a loser, and it's like they always said, I'm just a piece of garbage that has totally messed up her life and deserves this experience! With my luck, this is now going to happen again and again, and it serves me right!"

Now let's look at the same disappointment using the Conversation without Condemnation: (Out Loud)

"I know that I was treated unfairly in this real estate deal because there was a personality issue between me and the other agent on the transaction. I'm upset. I didn't deserve it, working as hard as I did. Good job, Karen. I'm proud of me, being this honest with me and feeling the pain."

"I feel really hurt! This is wrong!!! I'm concerned if this keeps going on that I won't be able to pay my rent!"

"Hmmm. Looks like one of my Museum States has been triggered. I better say the Powerfirmation for the Worrier: "Thank you, God, for helping me to see possible solutions and to focus on good outcomes for at least the next four hours. Good job Karen! I'm proud of me, and that's more God's success than mine!" "Are you ready to look at possible solutions?"

"I'm really tired; I want to take a nap, and then go work out. Then I'll be ready to look at my options for dealing with this problem."

"Sounds like a great plan, Karen. Good job! I'm proud of me and that's more God's success than mine!"

So after reading this short dialogue out loud, you can see the effectiveness and power in the Conversation without Condemnation. What you will accomplish with the Conversation without Condemnation is a more balanced and compassionate way of navigating situations in your life that contain fear spikes.

Write out a short list of situations you want to have a Conversation without Condemnation about. It would look something like this:

1. "Business has been slow this week, and I feel fear and anger."
2. "My girlfriend or boyfriend has been distant all week, and I'm afraid and angry."
3. "I'm feeling like I'm beginning to look old, and I'm feeling sad and afraid."

Write out your short list here:

_____

_____

Now, go to a quiet place and have a Conversation without Condemnation on at least one of these situations.

List at least one fear-spiked situation that improved by using the Conversation without Condemnation and how you feel about your success in using this tool.

Also, it's important for your building yourself up practice to share your Conversation without Condemnation with someone you trust.

I know that the Conversation without Condemnation may feel a little uncomfortable at first, but with practice it will become second nature to you. It may be the sanest way you've ever spoken to yourself while being upset. Isn't it crazy to hear in your head the unrelenting stream of criticism and abuse that you direct at yourself during a crisis? Furthermore, beating yourself up will do nothing to improve it. Remember, we can only stop something bad by replacing it with something good! So, think of this tool as doing reps at the gym. The more you do it, the stronger you will be. Like doing cardio and lifting weights, practicing the Conversation without Condemnation will build the "muscle and endurance" that will allow you the best result in those difficult moments that will happen in your life. The important thing is that you just do it!

Follow-Up Conversation without Condemnation

Later on, when you have cooled down, you may want to look at the situation again. You can have a follow-up to your initial Conversation without Condemnation. Here are some components you may want to include in your follow-up discussion.

1. It can be important for you to say: "What lesson can I learn from this situation? Good job for successfully asking that great question! (   )! I'm proud of me, and that's more God's success than mine!" Just by asking that question out loud without condemnation is a success – it's a good process. It will help you learn from your mistake. Remember, it's never a question of whether "you botched it or failed." It's always the simple question of "Have you replaced fear with faith?" Do you trust that God will help you to learn from this situation and create a new better reality?

2. You can ask yourself: "What choices do I have? How do I feel about these choices? Good job (   ). I'm proud of me, and that's more God's success than mine!" Then, make your decision. Remember "The best way out is through!" It is often better to take action, even imperfectly, than to escape or hide or isolate.

3. If at this juncture you are having difficulty with making a choice on what action feels right to take, then read Chapter 12, where I discuss "God GPS."

4. If you are angry and resentful toward others, it is important to let it go. As I said in Chapter 5, resentment is always a very bad choice: It's as if we're taking poison and hoping the other person dies!

Resentment toward others can spring from anything such as racist comments, being sexually objectified, bullied, condescended to, being reminded that we're "from the wrong side of the tracks," taken for granted, not considered, left out, demeaned, exploited, not acknowledged, or acknowledged in a negative manner, and "not being heard." When you sense that the person talking to you is "not really hearing you," that will cause you to see "eight shades of red that cannot be found on a color chart in any paint store on the planet earth!"

In order to release resentment, it's important to understand why we are resentful toward the offending person or institution. In particular, we need to see why we are so angry. It's usually because what the person or institution has done has created fear in us - fear of not getting what we want or need, or fear of losing what we have.

A solution to resentment that has worked well for me and my clients is to say a Powerfirmation for Releasing Resentment such as this: "I give up the right to resent (insert name of the person, e.g. Sharon.) May she or he have a great life, good health, joy and abundance! Good job, (   ) I'm proud of me, and that's more God's success than mine!" Why is it important to say "I give up the right" to resent him, her, or them? Well, we feel entitled to resent because of what *they did to us or didn't do for us!!!* So, isn't that our right? Sure, it is! But resentment is a waste of time, makes us miserable, and can hurt our health, so it's important to give up our right to resent.

Here are some examples of Powerfirmations for Releasing Resentment:

"I give up my right to resent Dan, for saying that my nose is so big that if I stuck my head outside a ship, it would turn around! May he have a great life, good health, joy and an equally abundant nose! Good job, (   ). I'm proud of me, and that's more God's success than mine!"

"God, thank you for allowing me to give up the right to resent Alexis for saying that: 'I'm as needy as her mother.' May she have a great life, good health, joy and abundance! Good job, (   ). I'm proud of me, and that's more God's success than mine!"

"I give up my right to resent my dog, Jake, for eating my boyfriend's T Bone steak!" Good job, (   ). I'm proud of me, and that's more God's success than mine!"

Now write out a Powerfirmation for Releasing Resentment

toward someone or something. It can be humorous or serious – it's up to you! Then say it out loud, share it with a friend, and write down how you feel.

Sometimes our day goes bat-shit crazy... Things are coming at us right and left... It could be a relationship that has ended, a legal notice that has arrived, or a project that is tanking. All these events will generate increased fear, which produces anger, anxiety and resentment. Again, it's the fear of losing what we have, or not getting what we want. When this happens, it is very important that we pause and take a deep breath. Then have the Conversation without Condemnation!

Chapter 10 Summary

- A deep expression of self -love is communicating relationally to ourselves by talking out loud to ourselves in a supportive way without beating ourselves up.
- When fear, anger and resentments are hurting us, it is easy to become reactive. Meaning, there is a good chance that we will take self-destructive actions if we don't talk about the situation with ourselves and build ourselves up unconditionally in the process.
- When we are reactive, we make snap decisions out of fear or survival. When we are relational, we take time to relate to ourselves regarding a decision, and the more relational we are, the better our decision.
- My suggestion is that you install in your walking-around

consciousness a "relational app," meaning, you talk things through out loud with kindness toward yourself as a new habit, knowing your daily focus is to go from fear to faith. The more you go from fear to faith, the more your life will improve.

- The important idea about relational communication is that it creates an immediate improved future. In short, it creates self-affirming actions instead of self-abusive actions.

- The Conversation without Condemnation is a conversation that you have with yourself after you experience an emotional upset, where you communicate relationally with honesty, kindness and constructive decision-making.

- There are several basic components to the Conversation without Condemnation.

- I recommend that you have the Conversation without Condemnation once or twice a day. It's important to do it as soon as possible after you feel anger, resentment or fear toward yourself or others.

- Later on when you have cooled down, you may want to look at the situation again. You can have a follow-up to your initial Conversation without Condemnation. There are different components included in the Follow-up Conversation without Condemnation. One of these components is the Powerfirmation for Releasing Resentment: "I give up the right to resent (insert name of the person). May she or he have a great life, good health, joy and abundance! Good job, (   ) I'm proud of me, and that's more

- God's success than mine!"

Chapter 11

Build a Relationship - Not a Reactiveship™!

There are two types of relationships. No, let me correct that. There is only one type of Relationship, but there are also Reactiveships™. That's the kind of being and interacting with ourselves and others that masquerades as an actual relationship but is based on reactive instead of relational behavior choices. One of the hallmarks of Reactiveships is that they involve very little conscious thought - sometimes none at all! They certainly involve feelings that are expressed, but with no attention to our gut feeling, and involve very little thought about ourselves and even less about the person we're having the Reactiveship with. Reactiveships mean that we're coming from fear rather than faith, and are blocking God's will. A Reactiveship is how we live with a minimum of conversation with ourselves and a maximum of actions. Reactiveships are filled with various Museum States. We sometimes even slide between Museum States such as The LessThaner and Crumbaholic to the Perfectionist and to the Panicker, and that's usually before breakfast!

A Relationship, on the other hand, is a state of spiritually feeling, speaking, thinking and interacting with ourselves, other people and animals. Relationships involve conscious thought and supportive communications with ourselves, other people, animals and most of all with God. It involves checking in with our gut, rather than overriding it. When we are in Relationship, we are coming from honesty, consideration and generosity toward ourselves and others.

To build ourselves up, we need to move from having Reactiveships to Relationships with ourselves and people in our lives. **How Do Reactiveships Begin?**

How do Reactiveships start? They start at home when we feel alone. They start when we're scared. They start when we learned how to survive. Trauma means receiving shock or injury emotionally or physically. When our childhood is filled with fear or trauma, we don't have the luxury of self-regard to care what our gut reaction is telling us, so we are like a pinball bouncing from one reactive decision to the next. Some of us were even specifically told by our parents or siblings that our gut feelings and decisions were not to be trusted. We may also have been told that what we thought and communicated was irrelvent! So, we got into the habit of not thinking and communicating, because "Why bother?"

On some level even before we have the vocabulary to define it, many of us know that we're in an unsane home. In my home, there was the mentally ill group and the religious orthodox judgmental committee. I had to deal with the unsanity of both camps, and folks, it was no day at the beach! It's been said that a child's mind is like a house with the front door open. Anything that occurs in the home is all about the child – the child believes that the bad that occurs is all his or her fault. So, we always take it personally when we are children. As a result, we often develop a Reactiveship bag of tricks that allowed us to survive. For me, I became far more reactive than relational at a very early age. Of course, I didn't really know what I was doing, but I made the choice to become a chameleon and a Pleaser on a moment-tomoment basis in order to survive in my family.

Was I self-centered? Yes! When you are mentally standing on "loose rocks," instead of on a firm ground, you're always checking your feet so you don't fall. The problem with this way of living is that I learned to disassociate from my gut feeling, and I did not know what I truly thought and believed. Also, it caused me to focus on me rather than the people around me.

If you like, you can pause now and write about the Reactiveships in your life and how they got started.

Please share your writing with a trusted friend, and listen to their writing as well.

Are you on Thinking Terms with Yourself?

Most of us think about thinking, if we think about it at all, as a process that occurs between our ears. To a degree that's true, but not always. Thinking can occur with prompts from what we experience, see and feel. It can also occur out loud. When I talk about being in a Reactiveship, instead of a Relationship with ourselves, the one big difference is thought. When we're reacting to our life, and making decisions from a place of zero thought, we're not on "thinking terms" with ourselves. However, I can hear you say, "it's not always possible or easy to think things through." You're right. Sometimes our minds are filled with so much noise that we can't even come up with a good Tweet!

That's why for some it's easier to "speak things through." What that does is generate two types of thinking - vocalized and subvocalized. By using Powerfirmations out loud, we generate both vocalized and subvocalized thinking. If we "speak things through," we are moving toward becoming more relational people who will be making better decisions than we did before when we acted first and regretted it later.

For decades I was always considered to be smart, but I never thought about my choices. So I was a smart guy living dumb, which is a classic example of how intelligence is not all it's cracked up to be. Now, by practicing Powerfirmations and not condemning myself, I'm thinking out loud and, in my head, and frequently checking my gut reaction, so I am making better decisions. Saying Powerfirmations gives us the ability to think about anything out loud with a strong spiritual energy supporting it.

Reactive Thoughts

Reactive thoughts are not really fully present thoughts, and they always are negative. If left unchecked, reactive thoughts lead to reactive behavior. They are thoughts that everyone has, but relational people will stop them so they don't act on them and destroy their relationships. Following are some examples of reactive thoughts that lead to reactive behavior.

"Screw it, I'm eating that! ("That" is always the thing that we will regret eating tomorrow!)

"With my luck, (   ) will happen."

"What chances do I have, my whole family is a bunch of

(   )."

"Hey, that guy is a total (   )."

"I was born on the wrong side of the tracks."

"All men are (   )!"

"All women are (   )!"

"He failed to come through for me this time. I only give a guy one chance and then I'm outta here!

"I've always been a (   )."

"She is so insulting to me; I'm thinking of going to the bar or bakery."

"I know after they see my performance, they will just criticize it."

"I never have the time to write, play, study, or teach. I just don't know where the day goes."

Relational Thoughts

Relational thoughts are positive, considerate and fully present. They can include Powerfirmations. Here are some examples:

"Wow, I have a craving to eat _____! What's going on with me? What fear is driving this?" Good job admitting my fear successfully (   ). I'm proud of me, and that's more God's success than mine!

"I'm worried that _____ will happen. Thank you, God, for helping me to see possible solutions and to focus on good outcomes. Good job (   ). I'm proud of me, and that's more God's success than mine!

"Thank you, God, for helping me to forgive (   ) for failing to come through for me this time. I know he has come through for me other times. Please help me to see him with new eyes. I give up my right to resent (   ). I'm proud of me, and that's more God's success than mine!

"Even though my family members were not successful, I have the capacity to create a new destiny for me based on a higher level of consciousness. Thank you God, for not allowing my past to determine my future. Good job (   ). I'm proud of me, and that's more God's success than mine!"

"I'm triggered by him/her, so I'm going to call a good friend to talk it over. Good job (   ). I'm proud of me, and that's more God's success than mine!"

"I know after they see my performance, they will give me a balanced review. I love to perform, and God is ultimately the producer." Good job (   ). I'm proud of me, and that's more God's success than mine!"

Reactiveship Behavior

Here are examples of my behavior from some of the Reactiveships™ I've been in.

The Anchovy Pizza Story

One day I volunteered to go out to get a pizza, since the pizzeria we selected didn't deliver. My girlfriend and her father wanted a large pizza. So far so good! Well, when I got to the pizzeria, I ordered anchovies, my favorite topping, as the topping over the whole pizza. I brought it back, and as my girlfriend and her father opened the box they looked at me in horror. They both hated anchovies and were stunned that I didn't consider asking them if they liked anchovies! There was no conscious thought in my decision, and certainly no conversation with myself or others on that day! That's why they threw the pizza at me, but I ducked, and it hit the wall, which amazingly resembled a Jackson Pollack painting! After this pizza become a modern art experience, my relationship with my girlfriend was not the same, and we never again went to see any modern art exhibitions!

Clearly, I am riffing at the end of this story, but sadly in reality the relationship was never the same. How different it would have been if I had been in a relational state and asking myself why I was making the choice to get anchovies. The truth was that I had some fear that caused buried anger toward my girlfriend and her father, and was not able to admit it to myself and deal with it directly. Instead, it came out in the anchovies!

Showing Up Late Story

Again, without consciously thinking or being relational with me in any way I had to pick up my girlfriend. I showed up two hours late. "She said angrily why didn't you call me?" I said "Well, I figured you'd know that I was stuck in traffic!" I wasn't thinking about myself and my choices and certainly was not thinking about my girlfriend! I was in Reactiveship City! What generated my reactive behavior? Well, it was my girlfriend's frequently insulting me, coupled with her wanting to marry me! This, of course, created fear for me. My fear generated anger and my behavior resulted, which was disrespectful both to me and to my girlfriend.

My point in referencing these stories is to give examples of the reactive choices I made in the past - always without being relational with me and the person I was involved with. Thank God, I am not the same person now! I now have a good relationship with myself and with my relatives and friends.

Now that you have some understanding of reactive behavior, please go ahead and write out examples of your past reactive behavior stories and tell them to a trusted friend:

_____

_____

_____

_____

_____

_____

_____

_____

_____

_____

(Feel free to attach additional pages)

Don't Override Your Gut Reaction!

How many relationships have you been in where you knew in your gut that it was the wrong person to be involved with, but you were physically attracted to them, or you were lonely, or they were wealthy, or they were socially or politically connected, or all of the above! So you overrode your gut and got involved with that person. Sooner or later you deeply regretted it. How many marriages, friendships, and business relationships have crashed and burned as a result of people overriding their gut reactions to get into those commitments – hundreds of thousands or millions?

Clearly it sounds simple. Don't override your gut reaction to the choices you make in your life! Well, why don't we go with our gut more often? As I said above, many of us learned to not do that when we were children, so it's easy to fall back into that old familiar pattern where we go with the emotional flavor of the moment – fear, lust, anger or ambition, often to our regret. We do this because it feels like home! There is a better way – get in touch with your belly barometer and see what images come to your mind. You'll see that it's safe to leave home!

Two Brains? Who Knew!

Scientific studies have shown that we have two brains: the big one in our head, and the little one in our gut. It's actually not that little, as it's comprised of more than a hundred million neurons. The little brain is always in communication with the big brain and that is why there are so many feelings that we experience below our belly button. Most of our emotional life is experienced in our belly and our stomach. That's because of all these neurons and the link up with our big brain. They're doing a lot more than digesting the burger or salad you just had! So "cutting to the chase," our gut reactions are based on the interactivity of our two brains. When you say "I have a hunch," there is a ton of brain and gut power behind that hunch.

In terms of your daily life navigation, there are two types of gut reactions that are crucial that you pay attention to: one is tension or a feeling of a knot in your belly. It means: Don't do it. Don't go there. Don't marry him or her. Don't take the job. The other is peace or belly relaxation. It means: Do it, go there, marry him or her, and show up on Monday for the job. It takes practice because other feelings can take our focus off our gut like lust, greed, fear, anxiety, and anger, but the more we respect our "belly barometer" and use it in our daily decisions, the better our lives will be!

Just God GPS It!

The God GPS is a powerful navigational tool I developed years ago. My clients and I use it regularly to make better and more authentic daily choices in their lives. They often use it in combination with the Conversation without Condemnation. Just like the GPS on your cell phone or in your car, it gives you the best course of direction in the moment. It's meditative, but don't worry! You don't have to learn any ancient mantras or sit crosslegged on a carpet listening to wind chimes tinkling unless, of course, you would like to do that. The great thing about this tool is that it helps us to tune into our gut reaction. Here are the simple steps to use God GPS.

1. Go to a quiet place and take a deep breath and relax. You may want to close your eyes. Find in your mind the most beautiful image in the world for you. For example, it could be a sunlit island, a field of flowers or perhaps a religious location.
2. Find an intermediate image, perhaps a beautiful island in the fog or the rain.
3. Choose a scary or ugly image. For me it's a fire-breathing dragon.
4. Now, for example, if you want to decide whether to visit a friend in another town or whether to practice your guitar, you simply say "God, if it's your will for me to visit my friend in this town, increase my desire for it. If it's not your will for me, then please decrease my desire for it!" A plain English version of this would be "God, if you would like me to visit my friend in this town, increase my desire for it. If you think the idea sucks, then please decrease my desire for it!"
5. Close your eyes and see which image of the three that you visualized comes to mind. If you are tuned in with your body, you will notice an alignment with your gut reaction. For example, if it is the wrong decision, you will see the ugly image in your mind and feel a negative gut reaction (i.e. tension or a pinch in your belly). If it's not the best decision, but not the worst decision, you will

see the intermediate image in your mind and will feel some uneasiness in your gut. If it's the right decision, you will see your beautiful image and feel a positive gut reaction (i.e. peace in your belly and you will have a satisfying exhale).

6. Now repeat steps 4 and 5 regarding practicing your guitar.

7. Say a Powerfirmation something like this: "Thank you, God, for helping me to feel and see what you want for me!"

You will now know what to do on a daily basis with greater assurance than ever before! When you are at the crossroads of a decision and want to know what direction to take, just "God GPS It," and that's always the way to go! I recommend that you use this tool twice a day so you become experienced with making decisions and it becomes second nature to you.

Just one more note on God GPS: When you first start practicing it, you may not be able to access your feeling in your gut, or perhaps you may alternatively not be able to see an image in your mind. Don't get discouraged! Starting with either the gut or the image check is a great beginning. You may also find that reading the next chapter will help you to see images in your mind.

Focusing on Your Gut Reaction Opens You to Having Intuitive Thoughts

There is another benefit to being relational by focusing on your gut reaction – you will be more open to having spiritual hunches (i.e. intuitive thoughts). Recently, I was scheduled to fly to Australia and for various reasons I was uneasy about the trip. The weekend before I left, I heard a voice in my head that said: "By Monday afternoon you will have an answer." "I said really?" I totally did not believe that I would have an answer about anything by Monday afternoon. Anyway, by three on Monday the phone rang, and I got the answer in a conversation with a good friend, which was to go to Australia. It was the most frenetic packing job I did in my life. It was also the most insane ride I have taken to the airport. I'm not making this up! It actually happened. If I had not been working hard at actually having a Relationship instead of a Reactiveship with me, I would've never heard that intuitive voice in my head.

Once you have an intuitive hunch, it's important that you do a gut check to see how you are feeling. I did do this gut check regarding my trip to Australia. Even though I was feeling anxious in my chest, I had a feeling of peace in my gut, so I trusted it. I also saw beautiful images when I thought of going to Australia. The visit to Australia was a great experience that was totally in alignment with the gut reaction and images that preceded it. Had I paid attention to my upper body feeling of anxiety, I would have missed a wonderful experience!

How to Find the God Voice Within You

Let's talk about the God voice in you. It isn't some stentorian voice that resounds in your head booming through a massive brain speaker system. No, it's a still small voice that requires you to get quiet to hear. It's accessible through meditating or just sitting quietly in a safe place and asking God for guidance. Now the thing to understand is that various unhealthy voices such as "The Prosecutor," "Condemner," and "The Slacker," etc. can show up in disguise as the God voice. The way to know the difference is that "the God voice" will never say anything that is hurtful, insulting, angry, or enabling to you. It's the difference between a quiet, loving, balanced voice and an extremely toxic one.

The God voice says things to me like: "It is done;" "Be present;" "You are not alone;" and "No fear; no need." It will <u>not</u> say: "Work to you drop;" "Eat a gallon of ice cream;" or "Rip off your customer!" Those voices come from us. Call it resistance, disease, the Yetzer Hara, the enemy within us, various unrecovered addictions, whatever. It just isn't God!

The God voice is accessible through meditating or just sitting quietly in a safe place, and asking to hear it. There is an old saying: "God will help if he were sought, not if he were thought!"

To seek the God voice in you, get into a quiet space and ask sincerely out loud to know what God wants you to do or be. If the voice response in your head is: "Binge watch on Netflix," that isn't it. If, for example, the voice says: "be here" or "be present," that is God's voice within you.

The funny thing is that the God voice has always been in us. Unfortunately, given the turbulent nature of our past, it was the last thing we wanted to hear. The amazing thing is that it's always been there and it's there right now in you!

Why don't you put this book down and give a listen! Try this exercise:

All you have to do is ask God out loud: "What is the most considerate and generous thing I can do for myself right now?" Then, just listen and write down what you hear.

Use God GPS for Thinking!

Why use God GPS for Thinking? Well thinking is a tricky process! Good thinking requires us to be in a non-condemning relational state. It has the objectivity of clarity and balance! Bad thinking has at its roots in fear and self-condemnation and can possibly lead to depression, anxiety and lying on your couch for many hours with a big bag of junk food looking at cat videos! How often have we been exhausted and mistakenly lapsed into a thought spasm about money or a charged emotional issue involving a family member or work colleague and felt worse, without a hint of how to move forward in a positive direction? The answer is more times than we can count!

In order to prevent this reactive thinking, I recommend that you use God GPS for Thinking to increase the amount of time that you are in a relational place with yourself. So here is how I suggest you work God GPS for Thinking. Let's say you're on the end of a long drive, and you feel fatigued or hungry! If you find the thoughts creeping into your mind regarding a highly-charged emotional issue involving money, love, your career, or politics, take a moment and say, "God, if it's your will for me to think about this problem now, increase my desire for it. If it's not your will for me, then please decrease my desire for it." Now, do a gut check and an image check to see what comes to your mind and belly. If you have a knotty feeling down there, and an ugly image, you now know it's not God's will for you to pursue that thinking at least at this time. It doesn't mean you shouldn't think about it later. In fact, later (especially after a good night's rest) might be a perfect time to think through the problem or situation. Of course, if you have a feeling of peace and your mental image is of a sunrise over a beautiful lake, the time to think it through is now!

God GPS for Creative Problem-Solving

Sometimes we are faced with difficult challenges in our lives that require creative problem-solving. Don't think it through; speak it through!

Here are the steps to take to use God GPS for Creative ProblemSolving.

1. If you are feeling fear or anger, you can say Powerfirmations for any small or big things that you have done, so that you build yourself up spiritually.
2. Do some information gathering. Then say a

Powerfirmation for your good information gathering.

3. Speak out each option and the advantages of it, and then use the God GSPS tool - see how you feel – tension or peace in your gut. Also, see what images come to mind.
4. If you still feel stuck after that, call a coach, therapist, or friend your trust and reason it out. [5]
5. If you get an answer in your conversation, then you can do an image and gut check again to make sure you are on the right course.

Persistence and Love within a Spiritual Condition

Persistence and love are commodities we have, but they are only as healthy as the spiritual condition that occurs within us. How often do we "love" the wrong person because they give us an allday pass into our Museum States? The same is true with work. If we're not in good spiritual condition, we can use the commodity of persistence in business environments that deliver very little in terms of income or quality of work experience. However, when we practice the art of building ourselves up without limits and help others to do the same, we are in an infinitely better spiritual condition. We then are able to make better choices as to where we put our love as well as what work we show up for. In short, when we are in good spiritual condition, we are more likely to build Relationships rather than Reactiveships.

Relationship Stories
No Socks Story at the Wedding

I was driving to a wedding from New York to Washington D.C. and was running late. All of a sudden, the traffic stopped. I mean zero movement. I didn't know it, but way up ahead a bus had caught on fire and firemen were spraying foam all over the highway. The

---

[5] I am available for individual coaching sessions. If you are interested in these sessions, please contact me through my email: **andrewdeutsch9@gmail.com** or through my website, which is andrewdeutsch.net.

clock was ticking, and the wedding ceremony was scheduled to start at 7:30 pm, and it was now 6:15 pm.

I was getting frantic texts like this from my cousin, the mother of the groom, who is like a sister to me: "Where are you?!!!" Well, I really didn't know where I was. I did know that the planet might be rotating in space, but the wheels of my car weren't! In terms of my relationship with me, I was being relational, so I was in a "no beating me up zone" regarding not leaving earlier. I spoke out loud the truth to myself and a friend: "This car is not a helicopter and at the moment I'm not able to control the situation, so I'll get there when I do." After a time that seemed like "forever on steroids," we slowly began to move, and the time now was 7 pm!

I got to the hotel at 7:25 pm. However, I had to change into a tuxedo, so after parking the car, I found a bathroom in the hotel and had to change there. It was now 7:28 pm. To my horror, I realized I left my black socks in the car, which was parked three blocks away! Let me stop at this point, and say again that in the past this would've been a great opportunity to beat myself up. I chose to instead build myself up - which wasn't easy - but possible. I had a choice, to be late to the wedding ceremony, or wear no socks. I chose no socks. Fortunately, the tuxedo pants were long enough to cover my bare ankles, so no one knew! Here I was at a wedding that cost a quarter of a million dollars without socks! Rushing through the hotel, I found the ballroom where the ceremony was being held and made it just in time. One of my friends still chuckles at how I danced for three hours without anyone noticing that I had no socks. At the end of the day (and it was the end of the day) it all worked out!

God GPS for Choosing Relationships

In order to create a relationship that builds you up, start by writing out a list of qualities that you want to see in a significant other, business partner, boss, employee, friend or pet.

Say a Powerfirmation for any of your Museum States that may

impede your ability to make a good choice.

Then look at potential options and apply the God GPS tool.

It's simple and it works well for me and for my clients!

Go ahead and try out this tool on a relationship you would like to develop. Write out the list of qualities you want to see in that person or animal, then write out your options, and use the God GPS tool.

Now share your writing and experience with a trusted friend.

Good job doing all the work in this chapter to build up your Relationships with you and with others! You are well on your way to having a great life!

Chapter 11 Summary

- A Reactiveship™ is a kind of being and interacting with ourselves and others that masquerades as an actual relationship but is based on reactive instead of relational behavior choices. A Reactiveship involves very little thought about ourselves and even less about the person we're having the Reactiveship with; we live with a minimum of conversation with ourselves and a maximum of actions. There is no attention to our gut feeling.
- A Relationship, on the other hand, is a state of spiritually feeling, speaking, thinking and interacting with ourselves, other people and animals. Relationships involve conscious thought and supportive communications with ourselves, other people, animals and most of all with God. It involves checking in with our gut, rather than overriding it.
- To build ourselves up, we need to move from having Reactiveships to Relationships with ourselves and people in our lives.
- In order to have a Relationship with ourselves, we need to be

on "thinking terms with ourselves." For some people, this is hard to do. By "speaking things through" with Powerfirmations," we generate vocal and sub-vocal thinking, which puts us on "thinking terms with ourselves."

- Relational thoughts are positive, considerate and fully present. They can include Powerfirmations.
- Reactive thoughts are not really fully present thoughts, and they always are negative. If left unchecked, reactive thoughts lead to reactive behavior. They are thoughts that everyone has, but relational people will stop them so they don't act on them and destroy their relationships.
- When you are at the crossroads of a decision and want to know what direction to take, just "God GPS It," and that's always the way to go! I recommend that you use this tool twice a day so you become experienced with making decisions and it becomes second nature to you.
- Use God GPS for Thinking when you are hungry or tired, in order to decide whether it's an appropriate time for you to think about a problem or difficult situation.
- You can God GPS for Creative Problem-Solving.
- Use God GPS and Powerfirmations for Choosing Relationships!

Chapter 12

Grow a Lush Spiritual Garden in Your Mind!

Growing a healthy, lush garden of thoughts and pictures is another great tool you can use to build yourself up without limits.

Going from Weedy Thoughts to Garden Thoughts

All of us have thoughts that we're not particularly proud of. In 1901, James Allen wrote an important book entitled "As a Man Thinkith." It's about facing up to the truth that, for the most part, what reality we wake up to is usually the result of our thinking. Every motivational book ever written has borrowed the ideas of Mr. Allen's work, usually without giving him any credit. So I'm saying here, James Allen, you rock! The idea that he proposed is that your mind is like a garden. It can be filled with weeds, or flowers and beautiful plants. Without proper gardening the weeds will take over your garden, stifling the growth of flowers and plants. With proper gardening, your mind too will flourish with "flowers and beautiful plants."

So, I've created a simple exercise to enable you to begin to get rid of the "weeds" and grow the "flowers." Before I get into it, let me just say there may be resistance in you to do this.

Weedy thoughts are negative thoughts that are focused on a bad outcome for you and possibly for others and often involve worry. Garden thoughts, on the other hand, are positive, focused on good outcomes, solutions, peace and prosperity for you and others. Weedy thoughts are usually created by fear, can be experienced as anger, and they happen in the blink of an eye. Garden thoughts are created by faith. So be patient, as a wise gardener would. If you can find a few Weedy Thoughts a day and remove and replace them with Garden Thoughts, that's great! Each time you do this replacement, say a Powerfirmation such as this: "Good job, ( ) for doing this garden thought replacement! I'm proud of me, and that's more God's success than mine."

Here's the exercise:

Step One: Get a pad of paper or iPad, and draw a line down the center of the page. On the left side of the page you will write down a heading called "Weedy Thoughts," and on the right side of the page, you will write down a heading called "Garden Thoughts." Or feel free to use the below worksheet in this book. **Step Two:** Write down one or more "Weedy Thoughts."

Step Three: Write down the "Garden Thoughts" that you choose to replace the "Weedy Thoughts."

Step Four: Read "your Weedy thoughts" and "Garden Thoughts" out loud to a buddy and commit to getting "the weeds out of your mind!" Below is an example of this exercise.

Build Yourself Up Without Limits

Weedy Thoughts	Garden Thoughts

1. "If that SOB doesn't sign the contract by next week, I'll just...."	1. "God, I know you've got this business deal in the palm of your hands. Good job ( )! I'm proud of me, and that's more God's success than mine!"
2. "I've asked her out, and she keeps blowing me off. With my luck, I'll be alone on the holidays!"	2. "Thank you, God, for giving me the clarity that she doesn't want to go out with me and the courage to ask out another girl who is a great person. Good job ( )! I'm proud of me, and that's more God's success than mine!"
3. "I've just stuck my foot in my mouth and asked an insensitive question. Why didn't I think before I spoke? I'm such a loser."	3. "I may not be perfect, but there's more good in me than bad! I'll try to think before I speak going forward. Good job ( )! I'm proud of me, and that's more God's success than mine!" God, I praise you for that!"

Weedy Thoughts	Garden Thoughts
4. "They have me over a barrel!"	4. "I have freedom of choice. It's time for me to get more quotes on the repair I need. It's an abundant world."
5. "One look at me, and they'll know I don't measure up!"	5. "I don't look perfect, but I am more than enough!"
6. "Some people are treating me with such disrespect at my work!"	6. "I know that some people are disrespectful toward me at my work. I now give up my right to resent them and, instead, I focus on the people at my work who appreciate me. Good job ( )! I'm proud of me, and that's more God's success than mine!"

Now, it's your turn. In doing this "gardening exercise," your positive relational thinking will begin to flourish as more "weeds" are removed and replaced with "flowers."

Weedy Thoughts	**Garden Thoughts**
1.	1.
2.	2.

3.

4.

5.

6.

3.

4.

5.

6.

Weedy Pictures and Garden Pictures

Weedy Pictures and Garden Pictures are images we have saved to the hard drive of our minds. They may be pictures from the past or pictures of the future. Weedy Pictures are always negative, based on fear, and focus on a bad past experience or a future that scares us. Garden Pictures are always positive, based on faith, and focus on a good past experience or a future we want to attract. Garden Pictures will create confidence, ease, peace and joy. If not replaced, Weedy Pictures will create misery, anxiety, worry and depression. Just like screenwriting back to a Museum State, Weedy Pictures will bring you back to being a Struggleaholic, LessThaner, Angst Glutton, and the list goes on.... Weedy Pictures differ from Screenwriting in that Screenwriting does not involve pictures – it is a script; it just creates a story.

Without consciously creating pictures of prosperity in your mind, it will have negative pictures, and there are primal reasons that your mind does this. For thousands of years our ancestors were concerned with survival. Worrying about a Tyrannosaurus Rex dinosaur sticking its head in your cave and having you for a high protein mid-afternoon snack was far more of your mental focus than getting a haircut!

Of course, we want better, so we're going to concentrate on creating Garden Pictures, which will help you avoid Weedy Actions and Inactions and create strong Garden Actions. The following are just suggestions, and to be sure, yours will be different, but they show the contrast clearly.

Weedy Pictures	**Garden Pictures**

1. Driving a car on skid row that is held together with chewing gum.	1. Driving your new sports car on a highway overlooking the ocean.
2. Walking in the forest alone and hungry.	2. Dining at a banquet with your family telling funny stories and laughing.
3. You and your family members being sick or infirm.	3. You and your family members being healthy and vibrant.
4. You living in a crappy space alone.	4. You living in a beautiful space with someone you love.
5. You working in three minimum wage jobs just to get by.	5. You being alive and happy in your chosen career which provides you with an abundant income.
6. Walking down an alley by yourself with a rat nipping at your heels.	6. Walking on the Champs-Elysées in Paris with someone you love.

Okay, you have the idea. Now list your Weedy Pictures and Garden Pictures in the chart below. The Weedy Pictures could be recurring or new. It doesn't matter, as long as you create strong Garden Pictures as replacements. They could be about the amount of money you want to make, your career and work, the partner you want to have, your physical condition, or the home you want to live in. It is important to memorize your Garden Pictures by visualizing them over and over so they can replace the Weedy Pictures your mind will "naturally" go to without doing this work. let's get started! You may draw by hand your Weedy Pictures and Garden Pictures, or cut and paste some photos in your Garden Pictures Page.

Weedy Pictures	**Garden Pictures**
1.	1.
2.	2.
3.	3.

Weedy Pictures	Garden Pictures
4.	4.
5.	5.

Now share your Weedy Pictures and Garden Pictures with a trusted friend.

If a Weedy Picture comes into your mind, take a deep breath, relax and immediately replace it with a Garden Picture! Then add "Good job, (   ) for doing my powerful image replacement! I'm proud of me, and that's more God's success than mine."

A Weedy Thought may occur to you without getting formed into a Weedy Picture. You can immediately transform that thought into a Garden Thought or a Garden Picture, as best you can! So, for example, you may start with the thought of a movie director rejecting you in an audition, but you need to replace it with a picture of you getting the part and then getting a standing ovation or winning an Oscar.

I suggest that you replace Weedy Pictures and Weedy Thoughts with Garden Pictures twice a day. It may seem difficult to do this at first, but keep practicing and it will get easier.

Going from Weedy Choices to Garden Choices

The pictures we put onto the "screen of our mind" all have one thing in common. They will determine the quality of the choices we make throughout the day.

Build Yourself Up Without Limits

Of course, if we're making choices based on wonderful Garden Pictures, there isn't a problem. On the other hand, if we're making our choices based on miserable Weedy Pictures, they will deteriorate the quality of our day. You can always visualize Garden Pictures that will change and improve the way you are feeling in the moment, and collectively will improve the choices you make during the day.

So, in the interest of getting specific, I'm going to show how what you have on the "screen of your mind" can choke off the joy and fulfillment of a day, a week, a year or even longer.

For example, there is a workshop on social media close to where you live, but you have received information that many of the people who will attend that workshop are much younger than you. Again, you experience fear - fear of what? It could be the fear of learning something new, or it could be the fear of being with people as peers who are young enough to be your children. So before signing up, your chosen "mind screen picture" could be the image of you being laughed at by these kids or you just not understanding the subject matter. If you don't replace this picture with you enjoying the process of learning, guess who is not going to the social media workshop? You!

Let's look at another common fear-producing experience: the singles event. It's the afternoon, and you can feel the resistance (fear) in your body. You compose a picture in your mind, perhaps in black and white, of you being unattractive and sitting alone in the restaurant. If you don't replace this picture with you having fun conversing with others at the event, guess who isn't going to the singles event? You!

Now what then happens if you don't replace the Weedy Pictures with Garden Pictures? Instead of you taking small risks and going to a social media workshop, and/or a singles event, you could easily end up spending wasted hours watching videos on people driving a jeep into a swimming pool and not feeling good about you! In your heart you know you made the wrong choice. By allowing fear to create miserable "mind pictures," you deprived yourself of these growth-producing opportunities. If, however, you chose faith and created wonderful "mind pictures," and took one or more of these risks, you gave yourself the opportunity to grow and feel good about you.

So how about doing this exercise?

List the Weedy Choices you made this month on the left side of the chart and the Garden Choices you made on the right side.

Weedy Choices

1.

2.

Garden Choices

1.

2.

Weedy Choices	Garden Choices
3.	3.
4.	4.
5.	5.

Now the best thing to do is share your Weedy Pictures and Garden Pictures with a trusted friend.

A Vigilant Gardener

For you to have greater piece of mind and positive energy for what is of value to you in life, the "weeding process" never ends. You must be a Vigilant Gardener. Just like a real gardener, we must look at our thoughts and images garden every day and remove any new "weedy thoughts and images" that seem to appear. They always will appear because they are created by fear. There are always things to scare us or there might be nothing there to scare us, but life can trigger a memory or mind picture that will create increased fear in us.

As I mentioned above, there may be times when you will face inner resistance to using this garden replacement tool For example, what do you do if you have a very powerful Weedy Picture coming through your mind and you're having a hard time replacing it with a Garden Picture, and your emotions are strongly leading you toward a Weedy Choice. You could say "God, I thank you for helping me to remove this Weedy Picture and replace it with a Garden Picture of good health, peace and prosperity. Good job (   )! I'm proud of me and that's more God's success than mine!" If that doesn't work, you could discuss your Weedy Picture immediately with a trusted friend, coach or counselor. One way that God communicates to us is through the kind words of other people. They help us to not beat ourselves up and to build ourselves up without limits.

Chapter 12 Summary

- Your mind is like a garden. It can be filled with weeds, or flowers and beautiful plants. Without proper gardening the weeds will take over your garden, stifling the growth of flowers and plants. With proper gardening, your mind too will flourish with "flowers and beautiful plants.

- Weedy thoughts are negative thoughts that are focused on a bad outcome for you and possibly for others. Garden thoughts, on the other hand, are positive, focused on good outcomes, solutions, peace and prosperity for you and others. Weedy thoughts are usually created by fear and Garden thoughts are created by faith. Our task is to find a few Weedy Thoughts a day and remove and replace them with Garden Thoughts as soon as they crop up.

- Weedy Pictures and Garden Pictures are images we have saved to the hard drive of our minds. They may be pictures from the past or pictures of the future. Weedy Pictures are always negative, based on fear, and focus on a bad past experience or a future that scares us. Garden Pictures are always positive, based on faith, and focus on a good past experience or a future we want to attract.

- Garden Pictures will create confidence, ease, peace and joy. If not replaced, Weedy Pictures will create misery, anxiety, worry and depression.
- It is important to memorize your Garden Pictures by visualizing them over and over so they can replace the Weedy Pictures your mind will "naturally" go to without doing this work.
- If a Weedy Picture comes into your mind, take a deep breath, relax and immediately replace it with a Garden Picture! I suggest you do this exercise twice a day.
- Weedy Pictures will deteriorate the quality of our day. You can always visualize Garden Pictures that will change and improve the way you are feeling in the moment, and collectively will improve the choices you make during the day.

- You must be a Vigilant Gardener. Just like a real gardener, we must look at our thoughts and images garden every day and remove any new "weedy thoughts and images" that seem to appear.

Chapter 13

Your Life with and Without Powerfirmations

You're beginning to "lose it" because traffic is slowing down. So now your adrenalin is flowing and perhaps you're having heart palpitations - all because there are a few slow-moving cars and trucks in front of you on the highway. Amazing, isn't it? To generate so much negative emotion about so little! This is, of course, road-rage. Even though you may not define it this way, it is really road-fear - fear of losing what you have (sticking to your schedule) and not getting what you want (the benefits of being on time instead of being a half hour late).

It's hard to be emotionally balanced during a moment like this, but this simple and common situation serves to illustrate an important point: If you can get this resentful, upset, and un-hinged at a few cars and trucks on the highway, what insanity could you unleash upon yourself, your family, clients, and employees over money, ambition, love, work, jobs, or politics?

We will discuss in this chapter some common life situations that will clearly show the difference in how they playout with or without using Powerfirmations. See how they relate to you. Have you been in situations like these? How did you deal with them before reading this book? In the following situations, I have placed the negative voices in the characters that would most likely come alive in your mind. You will see they are always triggered by fear!

Also, in the following examples, I will show that the impulse to beat yourself up never completely goes away, but with time *the power of building yourself up without limits grows.* Applying Powerfirmations in emotionally difficult and highly stressful situations will keep you on "level flight" and help you achieve a much more successful resolution of the situation.

If you have not yet read Chapters 9 and 10, where I introduced and explained how to use the various types of Powerfirmations, then please read those chapters now.

Life Situation 1

"OMG! It's Saturday. We're going out tonight, and my boyfriend didn't text me back!"

Without Powerfirmations

Okay, so you're "chillin" on a Saturday afternoon, and you text your boyfriend to check-in regarding the plans you have for tonight. You text him: "What's up?" No response. You wait a little while. Still nothing! You wonder if you should call him. You send another text which reads "looking forward to tonight!" Still nothing! You wonder, is he okay? You call his number and get voicemail. You wonder if he's speaking to his old girlfriend who you noticed is still on his Facebook page!

A voice in your head says: "He's with her. It's over!" The Red Neck Voice in your mind blurts out: "Why would he want you anyway? You're just low rent!" The Cruel Condemner voice in your head screams out: "He can go f… himself!"

Your mood goes from a relaxed laid-back state into a dark and worried melt-down. Before you know it, you're binge watching "The House of Cards" and eating deep-dish pizza. Your boyfriend calls at 5:00 pm, and before he can get one word out, you lay into him for not texting you back. He tries to explain that he was at the gym with friends and his phone was in his locker when she called and texted him, but you're still on the attack. He cancels the plans you both had, and the Prosecutor Voice in your mind says: "You deserve to be alone tonight!"

What happened? You inflicted so much suffering upon yourself that you unfairly blamed your boyfriend. You allowed your fear to morph into beating yourself up and damaged the relationship. You simply chose fear instead of faith.

With Powerfirmations

Okay, so you're "chillin" on a Saturday afternoon, and you text your boyfriend to check-in regarding the plans you have for tonight. You text him: "What's up?" No response. You wait a little while. Still nothing! You wonder if you should call him. You send another text which reads "looking forward to tonight!" Still nothing! You wonder, is he okay? You call him and get voicemail. You wonder if he's speaking to his old girlfriend who you noticed is still on his Facebook page!

A voice in your head says: "He's with her. It's over!" You say out loud: "Good job (   ) checking in with him. I'm proud of me, and that's more God's success than mine!"

The Redneck Voice in your mind blurts out: "Why would he want you anyway?" You respond out loud: "I'm a really good person and have a lot of love in me to give. Good job (   ). I'm proud of me for saying that to me, and that's more God's success than mine!"

The Cruel Condemner Voice might start to say something, but at this point you've generated so much positive spiritual energy about yourself that it will most likely "run out of steam!" You resist the temptation to numb out with pizza, or binge-watch "The House of Cards," and you instead go out for a walk at the beach.

Your boyfriend calls and you say: "Hi Honey. I tried to reach you, and you didn't respond. I'm concerned about you. Are you OK?" He explains that he's sorry but he was at the gym with his friends and his phone was in his locker when you texted and phoned him. You both discuss plans for the evening and have a wonderful romantic Saturday night.

What happened? You replaced the negative voices in your head with Powerfirmations. You allowed the positive spiritual energy created by Powerfirmations to become stronger than your fear. This protected your Relationship with your boyfriend and enabled it to grow. You always have the choice of faith or fear, and *you wisely chose faith!*

Life Situation 2

"My boss sent me a text, and he wants to see me first thing in the morning!"

Without Powerfirmations

It is 5 pm, you're about to leave the office and you get a text from your boss to be in his office at 8 am tomorrow. You think "Hmmmmm 8 am is early for him to have a meeting!" "Why?

What's up?" You anxiously ponder. "Am I being fired??"

The Cruel Condemning voice in your mind awakens and blurts out: "Your work sucks, and it's about time they found out what a fraud you are!" Your stress level increases and your thoughts darken. You call your wife and tell her: "Maybe he wants me there before others show up so there's no scene. What if the police will be there, and I'll be doing a prep-walk out to the squad car? Maybe my picture will be in the papers and everyone will see me. My mother at the home in Miami Beach will have a stroke! If my father was still alive, this would kill him again! I'll feel totally humiliated!"

Your wife tells you that it's probably nothing and there is no point in worrying. You tell her that you'll see her when you get home.

At the train station your Slacker Voice drones in your mind: "Dude, what you need is a stiff drink. Might as well get a buzz on." Five drinks later, you stagger onto the commuter train, and the Prosecutor Voice in your head pipes up with: "Of course he wants you gone. Look at you! You can't handle stress. You're getting old. Think you're tough? You're a paper-tiger."

You open the door to your house, walk in, and all your selfabuse and worry has taken its toll. Your wife, with stark concern etched upon her face, is wondering if she should drive you to the emergency room. The Cruel Condemner Voice booms in your head: "The loser has arrived!" Your kids look at you with fear in their eyes, the baby starts crying, and even the dog is upset. It's a cool evening, and you're sweating. You don't even have dinner. You go right to bed. Your sleep, however, is not good. The Lawyer Voice in your mind tells you "It's all over...sell the house! Your income will be inadequate to pay for the mortgage payments, and I encourage you to consider applying for public assistance and calling the realtor."

Next day, you have an emotional hangover. You're ten minutes late to work, your boss is a little angry, but takes one look at you and is very concerned. He tells you that he was thinking of promoting you, but he has to give it more thought...."

What happened? You allowed your fear to generate a terrible stream of screenwriting "what ifs" and mental images, which resulted in self-abusive behavior. This damaged your chances for promotion and created new fears in you regarding your job security.

With Powerfirmations

It is 5 pm, you're about to leave the office and you get a text from your boss to be in his office at 8 am tomorrow. You think "Hmmmmm, 8 am is early for him to have a meeting!" "Why?

What's up?" You anxiously ponder. "Am I being fired??"

The Cruel Condemning voice in your mind awakens and blurts out: "Your work sucks, and it's about time they found out what a fraud you are!" You say out loud "I deliver great value to my company and customers. Good job (   )! I'm proud of me, and that's more God's success than mine!"

Your stress level is still higher than usual at the end of the day's labor. You call your wife and tell her: "This is so unusual; I have no idea what this means. Is it good or bad? I don't know." Your wife says: "Don't worry! It will be alright." You say: "Maybe... and see you soon."

At the train station a Slacker Voice in your mind says: "Dude, what you need is a stiff drink. Might as well get a buzz on." You say out loud: "I'm great at navigating this work situation. Good job (   )! I'm proud of me, and that's more God's success than mine!" You instead have a soda - on the rocks!

Then you get on the train. Your Prosecutor Voice pipes up with: "Of course he wants you gone." You respond out loud: "I always go the extra mile in everything I do! Good job (   )! I'm proud of me, and that's more God's success than mine!"

You open the door to your house and walk in with a confident step. Your wife gives you a hug, and your kids jump all over you. Everyone is in a great mood, even your dog, who is recovering from just getting a flea bath! Next day you show up exactly at 8 am. Your boss greets you with a big smile and asks: "Would you like to run your own department at twice the salary?"

Life Situation 3

"I'm tempted to go off my diet again!!"

Without Powerfirmations

You've been overweight for years and tried many diets. You're on the verge of having bariatric surgery, but you want to give the latest diet one more attempt. Tonight, you're going out to dinner with an old college friend, who you haven't seen in years. It's sort of a celebration. You're on diet twenty-nine, or is it thirty? Well, whatever it is, you've made an iron-clad commitment to stick to it! Prior to showing up at the restaurant you told yourself that you are only going to have a salad with one scoop of cottage cheese and no more. You will not sink to "shameful indulgence" of being a two scooper! You have the power to push away that second scoop of cottage cheese! The strains of the national anthem are playing in your mind.

You meet at the restaurant and your friend, Paul, is a guy who has always been thin regardless of what he ate. He orders the biggest hamburger deluxe you've ever seen. The image of your single scoop of cottage cheese on an anemic salad flashes quickly and disturbingly in your mind.

The order arrives, and Paul's order isn't a quarter-pounder - it looks like a three-quarter pounder. Dude, it's a mega burger! It's dripping with cheddar cheese and jalapeños, with thick steak fries on the side and onion rings the size that would go through a bull's nose!

The Smothering Mother/Father Voice in your head says: "Sweetheart, eat; you'll start your diet tomorrow!" You change your order to a half-pound burger, topped with sautéed mushrooms, with a double order of fries on the side. Your food arrives, and a feeling of guilt and gloom comes over you as you devour your dinner. Your friend, Paul, sensing your upset, asks "Jane, what's wrong?' Depression is settling over you like the fog over San Francisco. You reply: "Oh, I'm fine." But you're not. The Prosecutor Voice in your head is saying: "Ha, the loser failed again!" The Redneck Voice sparks up in your mind: "Hey fat girl, why don't you order a banana split while you're at it?" To drown out this voice you order another beer, but the evening is lackluster, and you both know something is wrong. Of course, you never specifically define what that is, and like a thousand times before,

"it is swept under the rug."

What happened? You set up an expectation that you knew you couldn't fulfill, and beat yourself up again. You weren't honest with yourself and your friend. All of this lessened the possibility that you'd be seeing this old friend any time soon.

With Powerfirmations

You've been overweight for years and tried many diets. You're on the verge of having bariatric surgery, but you want to give the latest diet one more attempt. Tonight, you're going out to dinner with an old college friend, who you haven't seen in years. It's sort of a celebration. You're on diet twenty-nine, or is it thirty? Well, whatever it is, you've made an iron-clad commitment to stick to it! Prior to showing up at the restaurant you told yourself that you are only going to have a salad with one scoop of cottage cheese and no more. You say out loud: "Good job, Jane, just wanting to order the salad and cottage cheese. I'm proud of me and that's more God's success than mine!"

Something, however, feels a little off. You remember that your friend normally orders high carb burgers with buns, fries and onion rings. Now that you think of it, he actually won county fair burger eating contests three years in a row! You think: "How can I stay more in the spirit of the evening and not pig out?" You say out loud "Good job thinking out of the box, Jane. I'm proud of me, and that's more God's success than mine!"

So, you meet at the restaurant and your friend, Paul, ordered the biggest hamburger deluxe you've ever seen. It was almost as large as a Frisbee! It was topped with Canadian bacon, sautéed mushrooms and caramelized onions, with thick steak fries and onion rings on the side.

The Smothering Mother/Father Voice in your head says: "Sweetheart, eat. You'll start your diet tomorrow!" You ignore this toxic voice knowing it's up to no good! You decide to your order a burger, no bun, no fries, with sautéed tomatoes and caramelized onions. The Redneck Voice sparks up in your mind: "Hey fatso, why don't you order two while you're at it!" You cover your mouth so our friend can't hear you and say under your breath: "Good job, Jane, making this low-carb delicious decision! I'm proud of me, and that's more God's success than mine!" The order comes and a positive energy enhances the glow of old friends sharing a meal together.

What happened? You chose faith instead of fear. You were in a relationship with yourself and set up an expectation that you could fulfill, specific to the social event at hand, and didn't beat yourself up. You and Paul both had a good time, and you have increased the possibility that you'd be seeing this old friend soon!

Life Situation 4

"I have the urge to text my old girlfriend while driving!"

Without Powerfirmations

It's a beautiful spring day, and you're driving along the shoreline enjoying the scenery. You're looking forward to a softball game with some of your friends, and you get a text from an old girlfriend who just landed at your local airport. The Slacker Voice in your mind blurts out: "Dude, text her back before she goes out with someone else tonight!"

You override your gut reaction to pull the car over before you text her back, and start texting. Suddenly, you crash into a SUV. The cell phone flies out of your hand and your head slams against the windshield. You feel some blood on your forehead, and you know you've just totally screwed up! The Judge Voice in your head is awakened and pronouncing sentence: "You'll be jailed for this, and it is nothing less than you deserve!" Fearing the police will ask you for your cell phone and will check it and see you were texting at the time of the crash; you throw your cell phone into a nearby garbage can.

You are tempted to run, and the Redneck Voice says: "Hey lowlife, why don't you just die!" You open the door of your car, walking your most difficult steps of the day, and the Cruel Condemner Voice in your head screams out "you're a f-----n loser." You see that everyone in the other car is okay but stunned. There is massive damage to both vehicles. You and the driver of the other car look at each other in shock.

The police arrive and ask you for your cell phone. You lie and say you don't have it with you. The other cop looks into the garbage can closest to the crash and finds your cell phone. You're handcuffed and put in the back seat of the police car. As the police are driving away, your phone rings, and the cop sees it's the gal who you texted. He says: "Hey Romeo, should I tell her that you are unexpectedly otherwise engaged?"

What happened? You allowed the fear-driven Slacker Voice in you to make the mistake of texting, and then further condemned yourself for having made a decision which resulted in a serious accident. This deteriorated your overall state of being, causing your attempt to conceal the evidence and then being arrested.

With Powerfirmations

It's a beautiful spring day and you're driving along the shoreline enjoying the scenery. You're looking forward to a softball game with some of your friends, and you get a text from an old girlfriend, who just landed at your local airport. The Slacker Voice in your mind blurts out: "Dude, text her back before she goes out with someone else tonight!" You say a Powerfirmation: Good job being present while driving! I'm proud of me, and that's more God's success than mine!" You pull over to the side of the road, and you quickly text your old girlfriend. She texts you back and says that she is available to get together tonight.

What happened? You chose faith instead of fear. You said a Powerfirmation, which gave you the power to resist the urge to text while driving. You pulled over to the side of the road, then texted your old girlfriend, and are looking forward to a fun evening tonight.

Life Situation 5

You find a note in the kitchen stating that your wife wants a divorce.

Without Powerfirmations™

It is early morning. You go down to the kitchen, and you notice there's a note on the table. It reads: "I've had it. I want a divorce!" Your mood darkens, and your Prosecutor Voice says "that bitch!" Fear-driven anger and anxiety fill your body. The Judge Voice in your head proclaims "It's really your fault, Man!" You call her cell phone and get voicemail. You sit down, and hear from the Cruel Condemner voice: "Hey, you're a f----n loser, and you never deserved her anyway!"

You try to make some coffee, but your hands are shaking. You drop the glass pot, and it shatters on the floor. Your Redneck Voice screams out: "The loser dropped the pot!" You call your wife again. She answers. Your voice is trembling with hurt and rage. You say "why?" She answers: "You know why!" You respond: "We've got to talk!" She says: "We're done talking. I can't live like this! You will be hearing from my lawyer in a few days. In the meantime, I'll be staying with my sister." You scream: "You can't do this to me!" She replies: "To you! Do this to you? It's always been about you! It's never about "us!" Well, that's why this marriage is over!!" She hangs up the phone. You dial her back, and get voicemail. The Redneck Voice in your head says: "The marriage is over! Now no one will want you and your goanna be alone forever!"

You call your secretary and say you will not be in today. She says: "I was just about to call you. The boss asked me to tell you that there will be an important meeting with a new client and 'you have to be there.'" You reply that you're sick and get off the phone abruptly.

What happened? You allowed your fear to create a beating yourself up orgy, which you did not replace with Powerfirmations! This caused you to make a series of reactive decisions in interacting with your wife, based on fear. She responded with a final decision to get a divorce, and you responded with a decision to not go to work, which further complicated the situation.

With Powerfirmations

It is early morning. You go down to the kitchen, and you notice there's a note on the table. It reads: "I've had it. I want a divorce!" Your mood darkens and your Cruel Condemner Voice says: that bitch!" Fear-driven anger and anxiety fill your body. The Judge Voice in your head proclaims "It's really your fault, Man!" You know where this is going, so you cut this voice off and say out loud: "Good job standing in the kitchen focusing on this issue and building myself up unconditionally! I'm proud of me, and that's more God's success than mine! Hmmm. It was good that I've been often saying those Powerfirmations - this just reminded me of God. I wonder what God wants me to do, but I can't think clearly right now. Thank you, God, for handling this problem!"

The image of your friend Richard pops into your mind, since he is a good person, has a wife and knows both of you well. You reach him on his cell phone, read the note to him, and he tells you: "Be kind to yourself, Peter, and take it easy. We all make mistakes. Have you tried therapy – that's helped me." You say: "Well, we've been to ten marriage and family therapists and five psychologists, and none have helped!" Richard laughs and says: "The same thing happened to me and Susan, only we went through 17 therapists - in total! Then we went to a marriage and family therapist who also specialized in spiritual counseling and that worked! I got a counselor who is Jewish. I know you aren't Jewish, but maybe you can find a minister who is a marriage and family therapist. What do you think?" You respond: "I love Kathryn so much. I'll do anything to get her back. I'm willing to give it a try!"

You get off the phone, feeling better but somewhat anxious about calling a new therapist. Then you say out loud: "Thank you, God, for helping me to know that I am more than enough to find the right therapist this time! Good job, Peter. I'm proud of me, and that's more God's success than mine! God, I praise you for this!" You do an internet search and see that there are three ministers who are therapists in your area. You call up the first one, he answers the phone and you tell him your story. He says he has helped many couples who are in your situation.

You tried calling your wife and didn't reach her, so you leave her a voicemail message telling her Richard's story and that "I have spoken to a marriage and family counselor minister who has helped many couples that have been through the mill, like we have." You also tell her: "I love you, and will do anything to keep us together. Please give me one more chance!" You then say out loud to yourself: "Good job leaving Kathryn a great message, Peter! I'm proud of me and that's more God's success than mine!" You have a calm, peaceful feeling, knowing that you've done good work on your relationship with Kathryn.

Your secretary calls you and tells you that your boss asked her to let you know that there will be an important meeting today at 1 pm

Build Yourself Up Without Limits

with a new client and "you have to be there." You reply: "I'm on it, but I'm running a little late this morning. See you in an hour." You say to yourself: "Good job taking care of my responsibilities, Peter! I'm proud of me, and that's more God's success than mine!"

You had a very positive meeting with the new client, who signed retainer paperwork today, and received a voicemail message from your wife saying that she was willing to give it another chance.

What happened? You controlled your fear and limited your impulse to beat yourself up, down and sideways by building yourself up in a crisis situation. Your use of Powerfirmations allowed you to get back into faith and on "level flight." You called your friend, Richard, got excellent guidance, and you followed it. As a result of responding in a relational way toward yourself and your wife, you were able to make the right decision to go to work for an important meeting and you got your wife back, at least for one more try!

Life Situation 6

You are pulled over by a cop while driving.

Without Powerfirmations

The other day you got a new cell phone, and had not hooked up the blue tooth on the cell to the car's speaker system. The phone rang, you picked it up, and just as you did this, a New York State police officer noticed this and pulled you over. It was the usual, "license and registration please," and then he went back to his car to write up a ticket. Just as he was doing that the "Cruel Condemner Voice" in you had woken up and started with: "You will never be able to afford the fine, and it's your fault!"

You waited for the officer to return with the ticket. He did, and you took the summons and said sarcastically: "Glad, I could help you make your ticket quota today!" The officer then told you to step out of the car. He saw something in your pocket, and said he was going to have to "pat you down." Your neighbor, who is always sticking her nose into everyone's business, took a video of you getting searched by the cop. The Critical Father Voice in you then exclaimed: "The video will be posted all over social media, and your reputation will be in the 'cyber crapper!'"

Then you had a fear spike, which caused the Redneck Voice in your head to call you a name the equivalent of rodeo bull dung! All this was too much for you handle, and resulted in the longest binge-watch in Netflix history, along with consuming 15 liters of soda, 10 family sized bags of chips, 25 personal pizzas and more Chinese take-out than exists in Beijing!

What happened? You made a mistake and got pulled over by a cop, which caused you to get into fear and beat yourself up emotionally. This caused you to be sarcastic to the cop, which caused him to pat you down and be videoed by a nosy, gossipy neighbor. This generated a fear spike that caused the worst video and food binge in recorded history!

With Powerfirmations

The other day you got a new cell phone, and had not hooked up the blue tooth on the cell to the car's speaker system. The phone rang, you picked it up, and just as you did this, a New York State police officer noticed this and pulled you over. It was the usual, "license and registration please," and then the officer went back to his car to write up a ticket. Just as he was doing that, you had a fear spike and the "Cruel Condemner Voice" in you woke up and started with: "You will never be able to afford the fine, and it's your fault!" But since you have the tool of Powerfirmations, you said in the car out loud: "Good job, Robert, for having my license and registration at the ready! I'm proud of me, and that's more God's success than mine!"

You waited for the officer to return with your ticket. He did return and handed you the summons, and the officer told you that you need to pay the ticket by the date printed on it. You looked at the date, and felt a wave of relief, knowing that you will get your paycheck before the ticket is due.

You see your nosy neighbor turning the corner and walking her dog, and you say to yourself: "Good job, Robert, making this a very quick ticketing process, so my busybody neighbor didn't see it! I'm proud of me, and that's more God's success than mine!"

What happened? You knew clearly that you had been wrong in using your cell phone. In the face of making the mistake, you chose faith instead of fear, which resulted in building yourself up without limits. The positive spiritual energy you received from using Powerfirmations enabled you to successfully navigate the situation.

Your boss gives you a deadline that is highly unrealistic.

Life Situation 7
Without Powerfirmations

It's 4 pm, and you're having a meeting with your boss. He says: "Jim. I need you to prepare this report and email it to me to by 9 am tomorrow morning! I promised our client, Susana, that I would have it to her by noon tomorrow, and I need time to review it before I send it to her." You say to yourself: "Holy cow! I have plans with my wife tonight since it's our anniversary, and am just finishing a report for a different client that is due at 9 am tomorrow."

You have a fear spike, and the Prosecutor Voice in your head screams out: "You've been working too many hours trying to keep this job, and you keep cancelling plans with your wife. She's going to ask for a divorce, and she will be right to do it! If you say 'no' to your boss, he will rightfully fire you, because the company is in the middle of downsizing, and the employees are dropping like flies!" The Cruel Condemner Voice then pipes up with: "The loser is up against the wall again!"

In a hoarse voice you say "OK" to your boss. He responds with: "Are you feeling OK?" You say, "Yeah, sure. I'll get the report to you by 9 am." Afterwards, Jim says to himself, "You acted like a victim; you're such a people-pleasing wimp! The client could've waited. This is not emergency surgery! What am I going to tell my wife?"

You call your wife, and try to explain the situation to her. She is livid, and tells you that: "The only female you'll be sleeping with for the rest of the month, is our collie, Cindy! I'll be leaving a lint brush in the guestroom to take care of the dog hairs on your pajamas!"

What happened? You made a decision based on fear, rather than faith, and now have to live with the results of your choice. The only one in your house who is happy with the situation is your dog!

With Powerfirmations

It's 4 pm, and you're having a meeting with your boss. He says: "Jim. I need you to prepare this report and email it to me to by 9 am tomorrow morning! I promised our client, Susana, that I would have it to her by noon tomorrow, and I need time to review it before I send it to her." You say to yourself: "Holy cow! I have plans with my wife tonight since it's our anniversary, and am just finishing a report for a different client that is due at 9 am tomorrow."

You have a fear spike, and the Prosecutor Voice in your head screams out: "You've been working too many hours trying to keep this job, and you keep cancelling plans with your wife. She's going to ask for a divorce, and she will be right to do it! If you say 'no' to your boss, he will rightfully fire you, because the company is in the middle of downsizing, and the employees are dropping like flies!" The Cruel Condemner Voice then pipes up with: "The loser is up against the wall again!"

You realize that you need to immediately say a Powerfirmation, since you have lost your cool. You excuse yourself, and go to the restroom. You take a deep breath, and then say a Powerfirmation: "Thank you, God, for letting me know that the sky is where it's supposed to be, and you have me in the palm of your hand. You didn't take me this far to drop me! Good job, Jim, I'm proud of me, and that's more God's success than mine!" You feel the spiritual energy of the Powerfirmation moving through your body, giving you a blend of strength and peace.

You walk back into the office, and say to your boss in a calm, level tone: "Ted, I understand you told Susana that you were going to get her the report by noon tomorrow. I have plans with my wife to celebrate our anniversary tonight, and I'm concerned that if I cancel my plans so I can work late, it will affect our marriage. I could get the report to you by 3 pm tomorrow. Will that be OK?" Ted responds: "When I've cancelled anniversary plans with my wife .... Well, I'll just say that I cancelled an anniversary dinner 24 years ago, and I'm still hearing about it! So, I understand; I don't want to put you through what I've been through! I'll give Susana a call now." Ted gets the client's voicemail and says: "Susana, I know you prefer working with Jim, rather than other associates. He is available to prepare your report, but can't complete it until late tomorrow afternoon, so I'll review the report and email it to you tomorrow evening. As always, give me a call if you have any questions."

What happened? You chose to respond to your fear with faith and said a Powerfirmation, which gave you the spiritual energy to clear your mind and gave you a relaxed, yet confident, tone of voice and the appropriate words to say. Your boss then responded in the affirmative and also gave you important information – that you are well-liked by a key client. This increased your confidence in the security of your job position and enabled you to maintain your relationship with your wife and have a great evening!

These stories illustrate the qualitative difference in the characters' lives when they build themselves up without limits by using Powerfirmations, rather than beating themselves down when faced with life's challenges.

Illness or Injury

I'm including here a special section in this Chapter that is more extensively focused on issues of illness or injury because it needs extra attention.

Dealing with Physical Pain

Sometimes in life there are times when we have physical pain due to an illness or an injury. These times are not pleasant and no self-help book, no matter how brilliant, can totally alleviate these conditions. However, so much pain is based on different factors such as these:

Attention: Are you focusing a lot on your pain? Too much focus on pain can definitely increase the experience of pain. When we focus our attention on pleasant things, we are less likely to experience as much pain. Ever get so caught up in a game of touch football that you don't notice the pain of your injury until the game is over? On the other hand, if you fall off a ladder while you are painting the ceiling of your home, there will be no delay in your pain experience!

Expectations: If you are injured, what do you expect? In short, the more pain you expect, the more you'll get!

Emotions: Fear, anxiety, remorse, and depression, can amp up the experience of physical pain.

Coping Strategies: That's where we come in. There are many drug-free methods to reduce pain, such as meditation and EMDR. Powerfirmations for Healing Illness and Injury are a great coping tool for pain. Here are some examples:

"Thank you, God, for giving me serenity in my time of healing! Good job (   )! I'm proud of me and that's more God's success than mine! God, I praise you for this!"

"Thank you, God, for guiding my healing so I have a complete recovery! Good Job (   )! I'm proud of me and that's more your success than mine! God, I praise you for this!"

"Good job (   ) for remembering that self-care is God's care!

I'm proud of me, and that's more God's success than mine! God, I praise you for this!

"Thank you, God, for diminishing my pain! Good Job (   )!

I'm proud of me, and that's more God's success than mine! God,

I praise you for this!"

"Good job (   ) feeling the peace of spiritual energy! I'm proud of me, and that's more God's success than mine! God, I praise you for this!"

Making Decisions Out of Faith Regarding Illness and Injury

It is extremely important when you have an injury or serious illness that you build yourself up first with a Powerfirmation before making any decisions related to your healthcare.

Here is an example of a Powerfirmation which you can use before making healthcare choices: "Thank you, God, for showing me the appropriate steps for healing, giving me the strength to do the footwork, and letting me know that you have me in the palm of your hand. Good job (   )! I'm proud of me, and that's more God's success than mine! God, I praise you for this!!"

You can then use the God GPS tool to effectively make healthcare decisions in a way that is true to you

Powerfirmations for the Judge and Lawyer

There are situations in our lives where we are required to meet with a lawyer or have a court appearance, and there is a likelihood of a negative outcome. We sometimes are so anxious that we feel like we are losing our minds. These situations can often be turned around with Powerfirmations.

Here is a true story, which is an excellent example.

Last year, I was in Manhattan participating in a planning meeting for a conference. It was a Saturday afternoon, and in Manhattan on Saturdays many of the parking rules are relaxed, and you can actually park without spending money for a parking space. Anyway, when I came out of the meeting, I found that my car had been towed away! Thinking that I may have parked in an illegal parking spot, I went back to the location where I parked, and I triple-checked the parking regulation sign and saw that I had parked legally.

To make matters worse, I received a parking ticket on top of the $350.00 for the towing charge! My total cost for doing nothing wrong was $440.00.

After my blood pressure went down back to normal, I decided to contest the ticket and photographed the legal space on the street where I was parked. However, I was concerned because I couldn't really prove my car was parked in that specific spot since it had been towed before I could photograph it.

On the day of my hearing, I went to the Parking Violations Office in the Bronx (which is a borough connected to Manhattan). Let me tell you, the atmosphere of this office was not pleasant! As I sat down in the waiting room, I did a Powerfirmation for the judge I was going to see: "Thank you, God, for giving the judge I'm about see good health, peace and prosperity! Good job (   ).

I'm proud of me, and that's more God's success than mine!"

While sitting in his office, I showed him the photograph of the parking spot where I had parked and explained what happened. (I did not tell him that I suspected that the tow truck driver employed by Manhattan Parking Violations chose my car because it was parked at the corner and an easier car for him to tow to make his daily quota of cars!)

Believe it or not, even with the lack of proper evidence, the Parking Violations Judge decided to cancel the parking ticket, and arranged a refund of the $350.00 tow charge!!

So, prior to meeting with anyone who has decision-making power which could affect your life, it is mandatory that you say a Powerfirmation for that person!

Chapter 13 Summary

- The impulse to beat yourself up never completely goes away, but with time the power of building yourself up without limits grows. Applying Powerfirmations in emotionally difficult and highly stressful situations will keep you on "level flight" and help you achieve a much more successful resolution of the situation.
- Listening to toxic voices in your head can create disastrous Reactiveships with others.
- When we replace those toxic voices with Powerfirmations, the positive spiritual energy created by Powerfirmations becomes stronger than our fear, which protects our personal Relationships and enables them to grow.
- When we use Powerfirmations in response to our toxic voices, we greatly increase our ability to succeed in our work.
- A well-placed Powerfirmation at the right moment can even save you from getting into a major accident.
- As Life Situation 5 demonstrates, God can save an extremely difficult situation if God is sought and not thought! It's important in such situations to use Powerfirmations and possibly also Mini-Powerfirmations.
- As Life Situation 6 illustrates, remember to use Powerfirmations or Mini-powerfirmations if you get pulled over by a cop!
- Powerfirmations for healing illness and injury are a great coping tool for pain.
- It is extremely important when you have an injury or serious illness that you build yourself up first with a Powerfirmation before making any decisions related to your healthcare.

Chapter 14

Achieve Your Goals and Aspirations Using Powerfirmations!

I (And other Tools) had a conversation recently with my friend who had to give up coffee because it irritated her system. The only thing that would irritate my system would be to give up coffee!

This joke illustrates the importance of running all your goals – small, medium, or large - through your God GPS, so you only commit to goals that are true to you.

My clients often find that setting goals for all aspects of their lives is a rewarding experience. Some even create "vision boards" to remind them and inspire them to reach their goals.

In setting your goals it is essential to look at your talents and then decide what talents you want to develop further and share with others.
Share and Develop Your Talents

Thousands of years ago before dollars, euros and pounds, units of currency were measured in talents. They were measured in weight and were always precious metals of silver or gold. It's interesting and understandable that thousands of years later (meaning today) the word "talent" still exists but no longer has anything to do with gold or silver. Today, "talent" is strictly attributed to abilities in people. The connection to the ancient use of the word "talent" is the ability to excel in creating, performing or serving in a capacity that is valuable, as valuable as gold or silver.

Unfortunately, growing up we were often shamed or put down when we tried out our talents, and as a result, we decided to keep them "under wraps" for our life on this planet. I understand. The same thing happened to me. However, we have these talents for a reason. As I discussed in Chapter 8, these talents were given to us by God, and the more we utilize them in our lives and share them with others, the happier and richer we will be. Many of us have a dream to use our talents more fully, but somehow never get around to doing so.

My clients and I have found it helpful to do a Talent Inventory. So I'd like you to do a Talent Inventory, as well. If you are wondering at this point if you do have talents, the answer is yes, we all have talents! The goal is for you to own the talents you have and to give God most of the credit.

Before you begin your inventory, you may want to say a Powerfirmation like this: Thank you, God, for giving me clarity on what are my talents! Good job, (   )! I'm proud of me, and that's more God's success than mine! Now make a list of your talents, and how often you are using them and sharing them with others.

Talent Inventory

	Description	How Often Am I Using This Talent?	How Often Am I Sharing This Talent with Others?

			.
	Example 1: Playing guitar		
	Example 2: Cooking		
	Example 3: Mechanical work		
1			
2			
3			
4			
5			
6			
7			
	Description	**How Often Am I Using This Talent?**	**How Often Am I Sharing This Talent with Others?**

8			
9			
10			
11			
12			
13			
14			

When you have finished the list, make a plan with someone you trust to go over your Talents Inventory. Tell your friend: "My talents are more God's success than mine!" Then see if your friend will make a Talent Inventory and share it with you.

If you have listed a talent, and you are not sharing it with others, then perhaps you may want to plan to do that this week. Or you may want to utilize one or more of the talents that you have not used lately. It doesn't have to be anything over the top. For example, if you've got a talent for writing fiction and you have not done any writing for a while, write one paragraph sometime this week!

If you have a specific dream that involves a talent, then make a commitment to work for 30 minutes per day on achieving your dream. For example, if your dream has been to write a book, say a

Powerfirmation such as this: "God, thank you for letting me know I have talent and ability to write! Good job (   ) I'm proud of me, and that's more God's success than mine!" Then sit down for 30 minutes and start writing or typing away!

After completing your writing for today, say "Great job ( ) for successfully writing for 30 minutes. I'm proud of me, and that's more God's success than mine!"

So, what have you done? You've started (or restarted) a behavior based on faith vs. fear and used Powerformations ™ to spiritually power yourself through the 30-minute writing period, and acknowledged yourself, but gave God most of the credit.

It doesn't matter if the writing process was 30 minutes or three hours. Powerfirmations will work no matter what when you do your part and commit to this new powerful habit.

Remember, all talents are silver and gold in you, so bring out that wealth in yourself!

Just Change One Thing a Day

Some people have trouble with setting goals because they have doubts that they can achieve them. Positive change towards reaching a goal starts with wanting to be better than we are.

All you need for positive change is to do one new thing a day!

Change is as simple as that.

Let's say you haven't been working-out on a regular basis or even on an irregular basis and maybe less than that! You can make this one new change by using Powerfirmations.

Start each day with a Powerfirmation such as "God, thank you for giving me the inspiration and ability to work-out regularly! Good job ( )! I'm proud of me, and that's more God's success than mine!" Then say it again every 4 hours!

All of a sudden, you find yourself wanting to set a goal of having a regular exercise plan. You, then, create the plan and follow through.

So it is, and, instead of getting weaker each week, you are getting stronger, healthier and happier!

You grew into the habit of building yourself up instead of beating yourself up about your body and overall health. It started with one good new thing you did each day, saying a Powerfirmation four times a day, so can achieve your goal. In summary, if you want to achieve a goal, especially changing a behavior, create a Powerfirmation for accomplishing it by saying "Thank God, for giving me the inspiration and ability to achieve my goal (insert your goal)! Good job (   ). I'm proud of me, and that's more God's success than mine!" Then say it again every 4 hours!

Practice, practice, practice!

The Basis of Positive Change

The thing about change is that people do not know what they are talking about when they talk about change! Well to start, there are many parts of you that should not change! Your love of abstract art, kale smoothies, surfing, organic gardening, and dare I say it, clown face painting. When people ask you to change, they are usually referring to some personality trait, or behavior, that they feel is bothersome or irritating. In short, pissing them off! They may be very sincere in their request; however, they have no idea as to how that change is to be accomplished. Their "sad song" goes on year after year: "How come you don't change?" or "If you loved me, you'd change."

What's the answer? Our worst habits and behaviors are based on fear. Fear of losing what we have or not getting what we want. Going from fear to faith is a positive change that is essential to fueling other change and to achieve our goals. When someone asks

Build Yourself Up Without Limits

you to change, even though they don't usually know it, they really are asking you to go from fear to faith. Okay, how do you do this fear to faith switcheroo? Well, faith is a condition, a state of being. First, one has to earn it, and then maintain it - just like working out in the gym. To have faith without working for it daily is like saying: "I want to have six-pack abs, but I don't want to go to the gym and work out." No one in their right mind would ever believe that! Faith is the same way. Like doing cardio or weight training, it's a daily discipline.

How do we work daily - going from fear to faith? Well, if you have a major addition such as alcohol, drugs and gambling, the 12-Step programs of the world teach overcoming addictions with what is referred to as "working the Steps." This is a series of studies in admitting powerlessness over a negative recurring behavior, cleaning house in our relationships with ourselves and others, and trusting God or a Higher Power to remove the addiction. In this process, the message "faith without works is dead" is often heard.

If you are not addicted to anything like drugs, alcohol or gambling, you can still practice faith in your life every day. In fact, if you want to hold onto the discipline of building up yourself without limits, you have to give it away! *Faith (with works) starts with prayer or Powerfirmations™ and continues with helping someone and giving God most of the credit. If we do that, we will be given the gift of peace and connection.* Words like this will go with us throughout the day, "God, how can I be of service to you today? Who in your world needs my help?" This could be as simple as checking in daily or weekly with a friend on how you are both doing on making a change in your lives and doing Powerfirmations™ and other tools in this book.

Every morning, we're like an aircraft that takes off, and like a real aircraft, side winds will blow us off course. The winds of fear, in particular, will blow us off course, so we have to make fear to faith navigational corrections throughout the day. Fear tries to blow us off course; faith (with works) brings us back!

Overcoming Resistance to Change or Growth

There is so much resistance to positive change that it's a wonder that any positive change occurs at all! The reason for this resistance is fear, which causes us to take refuge in our Museum States, which also can be called "Home States." People would rather stay in a dysfunctional home, instead of leaving it, due to fear of change, taking risks, being visible, or simply being more alive! That's why it's essential to regularly do Powerfirmations ™ for Catching and Stopping Every Museum State and Powerfirmations to stop you from taking transit vehicles to your Museum States.

Here is a Powerfirmation that is also a good tool when you encounter resistance to change: "Thank you God, for guiding me to be of maximum service to you from this day to my last day. I know that you have me in the palm of your hand! Good job (   )! I'm proud of me, and that's more God's success than mine."

There are various ways that resistance can show-up in our lives. The discussion below indicates ways it can manifest and the solutions.

How Old Are You?

After 30, and on until 90 years of age, this question becomes very loaded. It has many implications as to where your life is at, what you accomplished, haven't accomplished, acquired or haven't acquired by whatever age you are. It is unfortunately a question that usually precedes judgment rather than a pleasant inquiry such as: "So where in Indiana were you born?"

What I've experienced with many of my clients is that they begin to use their chronological age as a basis of negative self-judgement: At my age I should've accomplished _____, and most of my friends are already _____. Then we use our age to limit the possibilities of our life.

The conversation usually goes like this: "So, Bob, how about getting that business, new career, etc. off the ground?" The response I'd get is: "Listen, I'm 58 years old, and at this point in my life, bla bla bla." So, Bob is using his chronological age to argue for his limitations. Are you?

Evelyn Waugh once said: "When we argue for our limitations, we get to keep them." Putting your age first is arguing for your limitations. Every day there are stories in the news about people who defy the odds by doing amazing things. What comes to mind out of recent news stories is the ninety-year-old man who makes custom braces for injured animals so they can run again; the ninety-two-year-old woman in Australia who is a power walker; and the seventy-six-year-old woman who is a power weight lifter, and I mean really heavy weights!

The one thing that sets these people apart from the masses is that they are not using their age to limit their lives.

All we are is consciousness, and we have earned it!

Every life lesson and realization, every accomplishment, every time we overcame a challenge, it's all a part of us. We have the scars, muscle and wisdom as a result of the years we have lived.

Own it! Value it!

If you are using your age to limit your life, start saying from today on, "I am the consciousness I've earned, and totally able. Good job (   ). I'm proud of me and that's more God's than mine!"

God, I Now Take the Limits Off of You!

Many times, we have a goal for ourselves that we are afraid we don't have the ability or worthiness to achieve. Due to this fear, we can easily trash the plans for the day by saying "I don't feel like it." This simple sentence has destroyed more dreams and lives coming to fruition than any other!

The important thing to remember is that even if there are some places that are good for you, such as an open mic, a networking event, an audition, a class, a jam session, or even a retreat, which would help you to evolve and grow, you most likely won't feel like doing it if you have a fear of failure, but walk through the fear and go and do it anyway. You'll be happy you did! If we do what we can do, God will do what we can't do!

This is especially true in any negotiations. When we sit down at the table to negotiate anything from a babysitting job to being on tour with a famous singer, our conscious mind is asking about hours, payment, working conditions, benefits, etc., which is all good. However, the curator within us of our various Museum States may be asking for a voice. Now, we may not know this consciously, but that doesn't matter; the Museum States are there anyway, influencing and defining our judgments and decisions at that moment in time.

For example, let's say you are sitting with your agent, and your goal is to get a favorable financial and healthy contract worked out for your performances. Your agent, however, is planning an arduous tour schedule with a "barely get-by" hotel and food allowance. If your Museum States are a LessThanner, Struggleaholic, Angst Glutton and a Crumbaholic, they are now fully alive and ready to agree to the deal.

Here's another example. Perhaps one of your dominant Museum States is being a Superhuman, Pleaser and Worrier, and at a family meeting the question is discussed as to who is going to devote the time to be a primary caregiver for an ailing relative. Although your goal is not to become the primary caregiver due to time constraints, you are tempted to take on the lion's share of the responsibility and resent the other family members who are wanting to "passing the buck" to you.

How do we get out of these situations? We say, "God, I take the limits off of you in this situation. Please go ahead and handle it!" Good job (   ). I'm proud of me and that's more God's success than mine!

God Loves Sloppy and Imperfect Actions

What do I mean? Well how about learning to walk? If your parents have a video of you taking those first few steps, you most likely didn't make it across the room. You might have fallen three times, knocked a few things over and scared the cat, but it didn't matter! You were so happy walking upright instead of crawling around that you got right back up again and gave it another try.

Do you have any old tapes or films in the attic of you using a spoon for the first time? Talk about sloppy! You had more spaghetti on your bib then in your mouth! How about taking the training wheels off your bike? You weren't exactly ready for the Tour de France. You probably fell off your bike enough times that your mom kept the local emergency room phone number on speed dial! However, learning to ride a two-wheeler without training wheels was so exhilarating that you kept at it.

What's my point? All of these rite-of-passage actions were highly imperfect, but you did them anyway. They were spiritual acts, as your spirit was uplifted by just pursuing them. You may not have perceived them as spiritual, but they were.

Perfectionism to me is a dirty word because it inhibits trying new things and taking healthy risks. In fact, in a way, we were better off as children, as many of us never thought about doing anything perfectly. We just said "I want to do this," and we did it. That's where you want to go back to - that innocent state of desire to follow your passion with no expectation of perfection. What is best for you to expect? Gradual improvement! Just like walking. The more you did it, the better you got.

If you were sloppy and wobbly learning to walk, and that turned out OK, why are you playing the Perfectionist in your life now? It's a Museum State that feels like home!

Perfectionism is a Museum State that is born out of fear of not being noticed by our parents or not being considered enough by our family, relatives, "friends" or teachers. How many people are afraid to sing because some relative criticized their singing? How many people are afraid to paint because some teacher denigrated their painting? The answer is millions! This is tragic because when we are criticized at a young age, we become Perfectionists and afraid to take risks, and our desire to create anything is cut off like an electric switch cuts off electricity.

Our parents then would say what's wrong? And we, as kids, said "nothing" out of fear that our parents would judge us and criticize us. Under the fear and the toxic voices in our heads, the desires to write, sing, play an instrument, act, dance, paint, or build, etc. are still there. They may be under the surface, but they are still alive in us.

Let's go back to that early period in your life where you said "I just wanna do it!" and you so you did it! Remember your excitement. Now, write out what you would like to do that you've been putting off for years.

1. _____
2. _____
3. _____
4. _____
5. _____

The idea that I suggest is that you begin something you have desired, do it sloppy and imperfectly, but enjoy the process and be ok with slow gradual improvement. Here are some examples of

Powerfirmations to help you generate some spiritual energy to make getting started easier. As always, say them out loud.

"I'm brilliant at learning to paint! Good job (   ). I'm proud of me, and that's more God's success than mine!"

"I'm getting better and better learning to play the saxophone! Good job (   ). I'm proud of me, and that's more God's success than mine!"

"I'm a great acting student! Good job (   ). I'm proud of me, and that's more God's success than mine!"

"I'm getting better at investing every day! Good job (   ). I'm proud of me, and that's more God's success than mine!" "Speaking in public for me is getting easier every day! Good job (   ). I'm proud of me, and that's more God's success than mine!"

"I'm getting better at writing songs every day! Good job (   ). I'm proud of me, and that's more God's success than mine!"

Notice in these Powerfirmations that I've focused on the process of awakening the desire to do the art, as well as the process of learning. There is nothing in them about mastery of the art.

So get that saxophone out of the basement, take a class, join a public speaking group, or go online and find a meet up group that relates to your interest, and when the fear-based voices come into your head that are trying to make you stay home, use a Mini-Conversation without Condemnation and a Powerfirmation to get your feet moving in the right direction. You owe it to yourself!

A Mini-Conversation without Condemnation and Powerfirmation used here can be as simple as saying to the kid inside you: "Hey (George), I understand that you are scared to go to the class, but I'm here with you, so let's go! Good job, (George). I'm proud of me, and that's more God's success than mine!"

The I Should Be Now Report Card

"I had expected that by this time I'd have, be, learned, gained, or lost _____, but I haven't." This created resistance in you to achieving your goals or even setting goals.

What happened? You didn't meet your expectations of what you expected of you, so you created an invisible report card and gave yourself a C or D, or even worse, an F. Why? You did it because you decided to set an expectation standard as to where you "should" be by a certain time. If that expectation hadn't been fulfilled, you started "shoulding" on yourself. Why? You did it because a wave of fear welled up in you to create plenty of motivation for you to return to your top three Museum States™, including the Perfectionist, the LessThaner™ and Mr or Ms. Guilty.

Can we let expectations go? Practically speaking no, and that's not really the point. What I'm saying is that "getting out the bat and whacking ourselves upside our head" is never a good idea about anything. One way to move from fear to faith is to acknowledge whatever progress we've made toward achieving a goal (even if it's just one-third of what our expectations were) and forgive ourselves for not doing more.

Here is an exercise that will help in bringing you back to emotional balance.

Write a Gratitude List and a Forgiveness List daily, in the morning, or at least, almost daily!

Why? Gratitude is an awareness and appreciation of what's good in your life. Forgiveness is taking the stones out of your shoe — letting go of anger or resentment toward yourself or others. It's as simple as that! Writing a Gratitude List and a Forgiveness List is a great way to make the transition from being asleep to being awake.

Ok, here's how I suggest you do it:

1. List four things you are grateful for, especially any progress you have made toward achieving your goals.

2. This is your Gratitude List.
3. List four people who you forgive and what you are forgiving them for. You can include yourself in this list.
4. This is your Forgiveness List.
5. Read the Forgiveness List out loud.
6. Then, read the Gratitude List out loud.
7. End with saying "And that's why I'm having a great day!" You are taking responsibility for how you want to begin your day on an emotional and spiritual basis. You're reprograming your subconscious for the day toward faith. That's why you're having a great day!

Now go ahead and give it a try:

My Gratitude List

1. _____
2. _____
3. _____
4. _____

My Forgiveness List

1. _____
2. _____
3. _____
4. _____

After you have done this exercise, I suggest that you say this Powerfirmation™: "Thank you, God, for allowing me to acknowledge my progress, even though it may not be perfect, because I know that it will give me the momentum for further progress. Good job ( ). I'm proud of me, and that's more God's success than mine!"

Preventive Powerfirmations

Build Yourself Up Without Limits

For years whenever I played the guitar some insult from the dark corner of my mind would well up and would demean the joy of playing, at best, or cause me to stop playing completely. It was as if there was the "parent from hell" in my mind whose sole intent was to insult me and stop me from expressing myself through this instrument. This is, of course, resistance on steroids! Resistance is always a force that everyone has to fight every day. However, if you come out of a trauma-based childhood like I did, resistance takes on a whole new power. Without replacing our hyper-critical voice with Powerfirmations, performing our art can be a daunting experience.

For example, I would start playing a song and if I made a mistake an insult would be disgorged into my conscious mind and pollute the experience. I couldn't tell anyone, but I for years suffered in silence.

What I found as an antidote to my self-criticism is to do Preventive Powerfirmations prior to any type of performance that can cause toxic mind blurts. These are examples of Preventative Powerfirmations:

Option A: "No insulting voices! Good job (   ).

I'm proud of me, and that's more God's success than mine!"

Option B: "I perform great! Good job (   ). I'm proud of me, and that's more God's success than mine!"

Option C: "Don't condemn me! Good job (   ). I'm proud of me, and that's more God's success than mine!"

Try this before your next experience where you had to duel with the toxic voice in your mind and see the difference! By using these Preventative Powerfirmations, the spiritual energy that you get by giving God most of the credit will work and be stronger than the hypercritical voice that wants to put you down. As I said earlier in this book, when we say "it's more God's success than mine," we're not saying it's all God's success. We are just giving God most of the credit! It's also important to remember to give yourself credit too by saying "Good job,

(   ), I'm proud of me."

Fear of Rejection by a Decision-Maker

One of the most common forms of resistance toward achieving our goals comes from the fear of rejection by a decision-maker. We are afraid to apply for the job, audition for the part, or call a person who we are attracted to because we don't want to be rejected, so we can stall and be late to our commitment or not keep it.

To prevent this from happening, I and my clients have found that in such situations it is essential that we say a Powerfirmation for the decision-maker. Here is an example:

"May the hiring manager who I will be meeting today have a beautiful life, with good health, peace and prosperity! Good job, ( )! I'm proud of me, and that's more God's success than mine!" What is prosperity?

You can also say a Powerfirmation for yourself such as: "God I turn this goal over to you. Please replace my fear with faith! I know you'll help me to succeed if I sincerely ask!

Good job (   )! I'm proud of me, and that's more God's success than mine!"

The Not Too Structured Daily Goals List

The Not Too Structured Daily Goals List will help you plan your day when your day is un-structured (i.e. no one such as an employer has structured it for you.) It is a time tool that will keep the day from getting away from you!

This tool will also help to prevent sand-trap thinking during or at the end of the day. As I discussed in Chapter 10, sand-trap thinking is going over and over a mistake in our mind and we don't see a solution or resolution. What worked well for me, and helped me to build myself up rather then beat myself down, was to have this "not too structured list" for the day. This List created clear evidence that I had accomplished something. It will help you to avoid the expectation trap! It is designed to take the pressure off of you!

This tool prevents the "fear/anger" tango that can often happen if your expectations are not met, and also enables you to set more realistic expectations. This tool is especially helpful if you are self-employed.

The Not Too Structured Daily Goals List is very simple and by looking at my sample below, you can see there are only approximate times written next to an action. The reason is that sometimes there are things that come up that we need to take care of. For example, you may need to pay a bill that you forgot to put on your List, or your phone might ring, and a friend is having a melt-down and wants to talk about a problem *that only you can solve.*

So, it's easy to create this List. Let's say you're writing a book on intergalactic speed-dating, and looking for a job. The way the List could look is as follows:

The Not Too Structured Daily Goals List: Monday

Write outline of first chapter of book on intergalactic speed-dating. (Approximately 2 hours)

Relax, eat lunch, and share it with your cat, dog, or both! (Approximately 1 hour)

Access job websites, fill-out applications and send out resumes. (Approximately 2 hours)

Prepare for job interview, including building yourself up with Powerfirmations! (Approximately 1 hour)

Go to job interview. (Approximately 3 hours)

Go for a walk and work out. (Approximately 1 hour)

Meet a good friend for dinner, and possibly discuss your feelings about your potential new employer. (Approximately 2 hours)

Do dishes (Approximately .5 hours)

You check off each item as you complete it. So, at the end of the day, you know what you accomplished. If you only did one-half or one-quarter of the goals on your List, or you were not able to devote as much time as you had hoped to a particular task, that's Ok. You are still awesome!

There may be times when you can't accomplish anything on the list due to circumstances beyond your control. For example, how often do you have an expectation to get a project completed by a deadline (don't you just hate that word) and are under high stress to get it done. Then, some larger event occurs such as the airport closing due to a storm, or your car dies and has to be towed, or there's a flood in your town, and every goal you have for your day is cancelled, done, over, tanked!

Now, you will likely feel anger or fear, followed by elevated stress, and perhaps some deflation. In order to get back into emotional balance, you will need to get into acceptance of this situation, and then, peace. You can do that by saying a Powerfirmation such as this: "God, thank you for allowing me to accept this situation and for providing me with clarity on how to handle it with balance. Good job (   )! I'm proud of me, and that's more God's success than mine!"

Please go ahead and create your own List. If you feel any resistance, indecision or overwhelm, then take one or two deep breaths and say a Powerfirmation such as: "Thank you, God, for giving me clarity on what you would like me to do <u>today</u>, and the willingness to do it. Good job ( )! I'm proud of me, and that's more

God's success than mine!" Faith = Willingness!

<u>My Not Too Structured Daily Goals List</u>

Date: _____

_____

_____

_____

_____

_____

_____

_____

_____

_____

_____

_____

If you like, you can share your List with a trusted friend, and see if they would like to do the same.

At the end of the day, you review your List and what you achieved. There's a great word that solves the problem of not getting everything done today. That word is: Tomorrow. That's why tomorrow was created: To continue what you worked on today! Whether or not you finished everything today that you planned, the one thing that's very important for you to say is: "Good job, ( ) for working hard today. I'm proud of me for accomplishing what I did, and that's more God's success than mine!"

When You Experience Hurdles in Reaching Your Goals

All goals, whether you writing a children's book, designing an App, or looking for a job, involve hundreds, if not thousands, of micro-actions and micro-decisions which create screw ups and breakthroughs that happen one day at a time. The important thing for you to remember is by building yourself up without limits, you might not always be joyful and feel like dancing, but you will be staying level. You will not be going down the rabbit hole.... As the saying goes, "Staying level always wins."

Celebrate with Powerfirmations When You Achieve Your Goal

We often struggle to accomplish many goals for months or even years, and when we do achieve a goal, we say, "no big deal, it wasn't that much of an accomplishment." The truth is, whatever you've done, required you to go through fear and your array of character voices and Museum States, tap into persistence, sacrifice, and most of all, have faith. When you achieve a goal, it's important to pause and celebrate your accomplishment by saying a Powerfirmation for Acknowledging the Small and Big Things We Do!

Chapter 14 Summary

- It is important to run all your goals – small, medium, or large - through your God GPS, so you only commit to goals that are true to you.
- In setting your goals it is essential to look at your talents and then decide what talents you want to develop further and share with others.
- Do a Talent Inventory and give God most of the credit!
- All you need for positive change is to do one new thing a day! You can make this change by using Powerfirmations

Build Yourself Up Without Limits

four times a day.

- The basis of positive change is going from fear to faith using prayer or Powerfirmations.
- The reason for resistance to change is fear, which causes us to take refuge in our Museum States.
- There are various ways that resistance can show up in our lives. There are solutions for each of these forms of resistance.
- If you are using your age to limit your life, start saying from today on, "I am the consciousness I've earned, and totally able. Good job (   )! I'm proud of me and that's more God's than mine!"
- There are some situations which cause us fear because we don't feel like we have what it takes to handle them. If we do what we can do, God will do what we can't do!
- God loves sloppy and imperfect actions. As children many of us never thought about doing anything perfectly. That's where you want to go back to - that innocent state of desire to follow your passion with no expectation of perfection.
- "The I Should Be Now Report Card" can stop us from pursuing our goals. One way to move away from this Report Card and go from fear to faith is to acknowledge whatever progress we've made toward achieving a goal and forgive ourselves for not doing more.
- An antidote to self-criticism is to do Preventive Powerfirmations prior to any type of performance that can cause toxic mind blurts.
- The Not Too Structured Daily Goals List will help you plan your day when your day is un-structured (i.e. no one such as an employer has structured it for you.) It is a time tool that will keep the day from getting away from you!
- When you achieve a goal, it's important to pause and celebrate your accomplishment by saying a Powerfirmation for Acknowledging the Small and Big Things We Do!

In Conclusion (for now)

I began writing this book on July 1, 2016. It has been, without a doubt, the longest effort I have put into any one project in my life. There were two burning motivations that powered the process over this period of time.

The first motivation was the ideas of Museum States, Powerfirmations and the Conversation without Condemnation, which I developed through working with my clients going back to 2014. I saw that these concepts worked and my clients' lives improved! Sometimes quickly, sometimes slowly, but their lives always got better, usually to the degree that they were able to commit to identifying their Museum States and using Powerfirmations regularly each day. The greatest joy for me is when a parent of a child or a partner in relationship would tell me "Thank you for bringing peace to our family." Or a mother would say "My daughter and I do Powerfirmations every day, and our relationship has never been better." These moments for me were, and continue to be, spiritual boosts that allowed me to continue to develop the work that is in this book.

The second motivation is that I wanted to give to the world the most accessible, simple explanation and tools to free people from the suffering they've imposed on themselves since the beginning of time. I truly believe the world would be an infinitely better place if all people built themselves up without limits. This will happen when one person at a time learns to use Powerfirmations and the other tools in this book when they are feeling fear. Perhaps that's you!

With much love and appreciation for your efforts, till the next time!

Andrew

Would you like Andrew to speak at your next event? Or would like Andrew to be your virtual coach?

Email Andrew at **andrewdeutsch9@gmail.com.**

Or Contact Andrew through his website andrewdeutsch.net.

**THE MOST IMPORTANT THING TO REMEMBER IS,
WHAT YOU HAVE LEARNED IN THIS BOOK
WILL FADE AWAY, UNLESS YOU GIVE IT AWAY!**

Printed in Great Britain
by Amazon